Lithic Analysis in Southwestern France

Middle Paleolithic assemblages from the site of La Quina

Susan L. Bierwirth

BAR International Series 633

1996

Published in 2019 by
BAR Publishing, Oxford

BAR International Series 633

Lithic Analysis in Southwestern France

© Susan L. Bierwirth and the Publisher 1996

ISBN 9780860548157 paperback
ISBN 9781407349404 e-book

DOI https://doi.org/10.30861/9780860548157

A catalogue record for this book is available from the British Library

This book is available at www.barpublishing.com

BAR Publishing is the trading name of British Archaeological Reports (Oxford) Ltd.
British Archaeological Reports was first incorporated in 1974 to publish the BAR
Series, International and British. In 1992 Hadrian Books Ltd became part of the BAR
group. This volume was originally published by Tempvs Reparatvm in conjunction
with British Archaeological Reports (Oxford) Ltd / Hadrian Books Ltd, the Series
principal publisher, in 1996. This present volume is published by BAR Publishing,
2019.

BAR
PUBLISHING

BAR titles are available from:

BAR Publishing
122 Banbury Rd, Oxford, OX2 7BP, UK
EMAIL   info@barpublishing.com
PHONE   +44 (0)1865 310431
FAX   +44 (0)1865 316916
www.barpublishing.com

TABLE OF CONTENTS

LIST OF ILLUSTRATIONS ii

LIST OF TABLES iii

ACKNOWLEDGEMENTS iv

I. INTRODUCTION 1

II. MOUSTERIAN LITHIC ASSEMBLAGES AND ANALYSIS 2
    Introduction 2
    Francois Bordes 2
    Chronological Variation. 2
    Functional Variation 3
    New Directions: Edge Morphology 3
    New Directions: Raw Material 4
    Conclusion 6

III. LA QUINA: THE SITE 7
    Geographical Position 7
    History of Excavation 7
    Dr. Henri-Martin. 7
        Stratigraphy 7
        Cultural Analysis 11
        Climatic Reconstruction and Site Use 11
    Germaine Henri-Martin 12
        Stratigraphy 12
        Cultural and Environmental Reconstruction 12
    Recent Excavations 14
        Stratigraphy 14
        Cultural and Environmental Reconstruction 18
        Sedimentology 18
        Faunal Identification 18
        Pollen Studies 20
        Climatic Reconstruction and Site Use 20
        Prehistoric Site Use 22
        Conclusion 22

IV. PROJECT RESEARCH DESIGN 24
    Introduction 24
    Middle Paleolithic Typology 24
    Limitations of Interpretation 24
    Lithic Analysis at La Quina 25
    Attributes 26
    Conclusion 27

V. LA QUINA LITHICS: INTRA-SITE VARIABILITY 29
    Introduction 29
    Artifact Class 29
    Raw Material 29
    Cortex 33
    Cortex Position 33
    Angle of Deviation 33
    Flake Morphology 36
    Exterior Flake Scars 36
    Platform Morphology: Cortex 36
    Platform Surface 36
    Reduction Technique 40
    Retouched Artifacts: Tool Typology 40

Flakes of Manufacture and Retouch 44
Retouch Intensity 45
Metric Observations: Flake Size 45
Breakage 48
Weight 53
Burned Flakes 53
Conclusion 53

VI. INTERPRETATION OF LITHIC VARIABILITY 58
Introduction 58
Analysis by Stratum 58
Cultural Patterns 60
Conclusion 61

VII. CONCLUSION 62

APPENDIX I: LA QUINA DATA ENTRY PROGRAM 66

APPENDIX II: ATTRIBUTE DESCRIPTIONS 68

REFERENCES 69

LIST OF ILLUSTRATIONS

Figure   Page

1. Map of France and location of La Quina 8
2. Contour map of Voultron Valley 9
3. Plan of La Quina (1923) 10
4. La Quina profile (1923) 10
5. La Quina profile (1969) 13
6. Plan of La Quina excavations (1991) 13
7. Profile of upper beds 15
8. Profile of lower and middle beds 15
9. Schematic profile 16
10. Stages of burning of bone fragments graded by size 19
11. Isometric diagram of structure ST1 19

LIST OF TABLES

Table   Page

1. Artifacts by Class 30
2. Artifacts by Class by Location 30
3. Raw Material 30
4. Quartz Artifacts 31
5. Raw Material by Location 31
6. Raw Material: Column Samples. 32
7. Cortex 32
8. Cortex: Flake Bags 34
9. Cortex: Column Samples 34
10. Cortex by Location 34
11. Cortex Position 35
12. Angle of Deviation 35
13. Flake Shape 37
14. Flake Thickness 37
15. Flake Scars 38
16. Platform Cortex 38
17. Platform Surface 39
18. Core Reduction 41
19. Cores 41
20. Kombewa/Janus Flakes 41
21. Retouched Flake Tools 42
22. Other Tools. 42
23. Major Tool Groups 42
24. Reduction Intensity Ratio: Scrapers 43
25. Reduction Intensity Ratio: Notched Tools 43
26. Retouch Flakes 43
27. Retouch Flakes by Bed 46
28. Retouch Intensity 46
29. Tool and Flake Length 47
30. Tool and Flake Width 49
31. Tool and Flake Thickness 50
32. Width/Thickness Ratio: Tools and Flakes 50
33. Tool and Flake Length by Location 51
34. Tool and Flake Width by Location 51
35. Tool and Flake Thickness by Location 52
36. Flake Size: Column Samples 52
37. Breakage 54
38. Breakage: Flake Bags. 54
39. Breakage: Column Samples 55
40. Breakage by Location 55
41. Material by Weight in Grams: Column Samples. 56
42. Burned Flakes: Flake Bags 56

ACKNOWLEDGEMENTS

This analysis of the lithics from the site of La Quina (Charente) was the basis for my doctoral thesis. As always, the fulfillment of a doctoral degree is guided by many people. Three people in particular gave direction to my archaeological career. Junius Bird taught me how to look at lithic remains and stayed with me in spirit throughout the doctoral process. David Hurst Thomas gave me my first taste of field work more than twenty years ago and has remained a friend and mentor for many years. Arthur Jelinek pointed the way through six years of graduate school and provided me with the idea for this project as well as the opportunity to execute the work at La Quina.

My extended family of friends and relatives were immeasurably supportive thoughout my years in graduate school. Their love and belief in me made the task bearable and sometimes even enjoyable.

I would also like to thank my crews and associates in France. The La Quina excavations would not have progressed without their time and tolerance, especially that of Andre Debenath. Generous permission to view the collections of François Bordes was given by Madame de Sonneville-Bordes. I would also like to acknowledge the assistance of my dissertation committee; Arthur Jelinek, Paul Fish, and John Olsen. Finally, Barb Roth spent many hours reading and editing drafts of my thesis and helped with revisions for this volume. Dennis O'Brien supplied the finishing touches with his maps and illustrations.

Many thanks to all.

Susan L. Bierwirth
Healdsburg, CA
December 1995

CHAPTER I

INTRODUCTION

This analysis of lithic remains from the site of La Quina in the Charente region of France was undertaken to add to the understanding of Neanderthal technology and subsistence behavior. Middle Paleolithic studies have been hampered until recently by a limited recovered sample of Neanderthal fossils and a lack of absolute dating techniques for this period. The durability of stone has meant that lithic artifacts, especially retouched tools, from Mousterian assemblages have been at the center of almost all of these analyses. While typology was central to most of this earlier research, recent studies have focused less on individual tool types and more on continuity in tool morphology. The availability of raw material and environmental factors have also recently been tied to lithic variability in the Middle Paleolithic. This study integrates analyses of the retouched tools from a series of beds at La Quina with the all of the remaining lithic artifacts in the assemblages. Analysis of the full lithic component from these beds presents new insights into variability in tool morphology, technology, and reduction intensity. The variation in these three aspects of lithic technology is correlated with raw material acquisition and patterns of mobility.

The site of La Quina lies at the northern extreme of the Dordogne drainage basin in Southwest France. The cultural material was deposited in a wedge of sediments stretching 100 meters along the base of a limestone cliff. These sediments extend more than 15 meters from the cliff face at their base and reach a height of more than 7 meters. The series of geological and archaeological strata was first discovered at the end of the nineteenth century. A large portion of the site was removed by Dr. Henri-Martin and by his daughter in excavations during the first half of this century. They recovered partial remains of more than twenty Neanderthals associated with quantities of animal bone and numbers of retouched flint artifacts. They found numerous heavily reduced scrapers that are now known as Quina scrapers (Bordes 1961).

As the locus for which Quina Mousterian assemblages are named, this locale has played an important role in the comprehension of Middle Paleolithic culture history. Yet the context of the La Quina lithic assemblages has been poorly understood. In 1985 a cooperative international project led by Arthur Jelinek (University of Arizona), André Debénath (University of Bordeaux), and Harold Dibble (University of Pennsylvania) was begun. These excavations were undertaken to refine the geology and chronology of the sediments at La Quina as well as to clarify interpretations of cultural activity at the site over time. The high resolution of the current excavations provides an important new sample of cultural materials.

The lithic sample for this analysis was recovered during the six years that the writer was involved with the La Quina project (1985-1990). Material from thirteen geologically-defined beds was sampled. All artifacts over 3 cm were analyzed in detail. Smaller lithic objects with evidence of specific core preparation or tool manufacture were also examined in detail. Sixteen attributes were recorded on a total of 6392 artifacts, including 1162 retouched tools, in order to discern patterns of technological and morphological variation. More than ten thousand small flakes were counted and sorted by material, completeness, and cortical cover.

Comparisons of attribute frequencies between the strata at La Quina were used to discern variation in Middle Paleolithic stone technology and typology. Variability in stages of lithic manufacture, technique of reduction, and reduction intensity as well as variability in tool morphology were recognized in this analysis. Two sets of associated materials are repeatedly found. Scrapers are associated only with late stage reduction debris and generally occur in opposition to denticulate and notched tools and early stage reduction debris. The latter assemblages also show more variability in tool form and reduction technique than the scraper-rich assemblages. Much of the variation in these lithic materials is suggested to be related to raw material availability and reduction intensity. These factors are in turn tied to environmental constraints, settlement, and economy in the Middle Paleolithic.

The analysis of the lithics at La Quina presented here demonstrates a likelihood of planning in lithic procurement for this context. Evidence from other archaeological loci have shown similar patterns of resource use continuing from the Middle to the Upper Paleolithic. Thus, many present interpretations of differences between Neanderthals and anatomically modern humans may be more heavily grounded in history than in science.

CHAPTER II

MOUSTERIAN LITHIC ASSEMBLAGE VARIABILITY

Introduction

Artifacts from early Upper Pleistocene deposits are most frequently defined as Mousterian assemblages under the cultural heading of the Middle Paleolithic. Only the "classic" Mousterian assemblages of Europe and Southwest Asia are considered in this chapter, although industries from the Middle Paleolithic of Africa and Asia exhibiting similar reduction techniques and tool morphology have been considered analogous to Mousterian industries (Chang 1986, Clark and Kleindienst 1974, Wu and Olsen 1985). Many of these other industries may be culturally related in a broad sense to the Western European Mousterian, but they are technologically distinctive when compared to the assemblages from La Quina. Even the lithic industries of Southwest Asia, which appear technologically similar to Western European industries, may be considered to reflect a discrete cultural tradition.

"Classic" Mousterian assemblages are found in Europe and Southwest Asia from approximately 125,000 years ago, the Riss-Würm interglacial. The last Mousterian assemblages are found in Western Europe at approximately 35,000 years ago, the Würm II/III interstadial. This period has been correlated with oxygen isotope stages 5e-3 (Shackleton and Opdyke 1973; Laville 1988). Unfortunately, the period falls in between the known ranges of potassium/argon and carbon dating techniques. Although new dating techniques (i.e. Electronic Spin Resonance and thermoluminescence) may soon accurately date these industries, a near absence of absolute dates for the Middle Paleolithic has made investigation and correlation of these assemblages extremely difficult. The lack of chronological control for Mousterian lithic assemblages has led to problems in understanding Middle Paleolithic cultural development as well as its relationship to human biological evolution. The association of Neanderthals, *Homo sapiens neanderthalensis*, and Middle Paleolithic assemblages seems to be undisputed for Western European assemblages. This exclusive cultural and biological association is less clear for the remains of Middle Paleolithic sites of the Southwest Asia (Jelinek 1982b, 1990b).

François Bordes

By the second half of the nineteenth century, humans were understood by European scientists to have coexisted with extinct mammals as evidenced by the stone tools they left associated with the animal bones (Grayson 1983). Excavations and analyses by Henry Christy and Edouard Lartet (1864) introduced relative chronology based upon paleontological data to these early studies of European archaeology (Daniel 1950). Gabriel de Mortillet (1883), the Abbe Henri Breuil (1913), and Denis Peyrony (1934) relied upon technological change rather than faunal variation to segregate assemblages from the European Paleolithic. They emphasized the evolutionary nature of cultural change. For nearly one hundred years, this evolutionary perspective remained at the center of most archaeological research.

For the last half-century, the archaeological perspective of

François Bordes has dominated French Paleolithic studies . Bordes was schooled in a tradition of cultural evolution, particularly the views of Breuil and Peyrony, but Bordes' work marked a clear departure from the view held by his predecessors. His comparative approach demanded comparable results from a wide range of site locales and regions. For Bordes, the keys to documenting variability in Middle Paleolithic assemblages were technology, quantification, and site stratigraphy. Bordes' indices for lithic reduction techniques and classification of retouched tools based upon repetition of form are still widely used (Bordes 1950a). With Maurice Bourgon, Bordes synthesized data from a number of French Mousterian assemblages (1951). They used and expanded upon Bordes' earlier classification and found that they could define four variants of Mousterian assemblages: Mousterian of Acheulean Tradition, Denticulate Mousterian, Typical Mousterian and Charentian Mousterian. Each of these Mousterian variants was distinguished by the dominance, presence, or absence of certain tool forms.

Typical Mousterian assemblages included a mixture of various tool types including both scrapers and notched or denticulate tools with no bifaces. The Mousterian of Acheulean Tradition (MTA) assemblages each included several bifaces and evidence of bifacial reduction along with a variety of tools similar to those found in Typical Mousterian assemblages. Assemblages with higher frequencies of bifaces and scrapers were called MTA Type A, while assemblages with fewer bifaces and more denticulate or notched pieces than scrapers were characterized as MTA Type B industries. Scraper-rich assemblages were grouped by Bordes and Bourgon under the heading of Charentian Mousterian. Quina Mousterian assemblages were dominated by thick scrapers with little evidence of Levallois production. In contrast, Ferrassie Mousterian assemblages were dominated by scrapers, but the index of Levallois technique was high and the scrapers were thin. The final Mousterian variant recognized by Bordes and Bourgon joined industries with high frequencies of denticulate and notched tools. These assemblages were classified as Denticulate Mousterian.

Bordes continued for many years refining his typology and searching for causes of variability in the occurrence of these Mousterian variants (Bordes 1961, 1966, 1968, 1972; Bordes and de Sonneville-Bordes 1970). He thought that the repetition of tool forms and assemblage types was too distinctly patterned to represent chance occurrence and that the variants appeared to exist over a long period of time with little change. Retaining some of his evolutionary perspective, Bordes believed that Mousterian lithic variation was the result of cultural differences. Given the low population of Western Europe during the Early Würm, he argued that it was possible that different peoples had coexisted for thousands of years without influencing each other's material culture.

Chronological Variation

The absence of absolute dates for the Middle Paleolithic led

Paul Mellars (1969, 1970) to examine relative chronologies within a number of Mousterian sites. Mellars found that some of the industrial variants defined by Bordes (1968) revealed chronological patterning. When found together, Mousterian of Acheulean Tradition (MTA) industries always overlay Quina or Ferrassie industries. Within the MTA, Bordes and Mellars agreed that some evolution had occurred with directional changes in tool frequencies between MTA-A and MTA-B. Mellars also believed that he saw gradual evolution in the decreased use of the Levallois technique between Ferrassie and Quina industries.

In an attempt to resolve this question, Bordes worked with his pupil, Henri Laville to develop relative geological and environmental sequences for excavated sites in Southwest France. Laville (1964, 1975, 1988; Laville *et al.* 1980) used sedimentological analysis to compare and seriate the sequences from a number of sites in the Périgord. Laville used analysis of the sediments, especially limestone fragments (*eboulis*), to discern relative changes in temperature and moisture. His climatic correlations and chronology indicated that any Mousterian variant could have existed at any time. These findings appeared to confirm Bordes cultural explanation for typological variation. Bordes and Laville also agreed that deposition of the Mousterian variants did not correspond to any specific season or climatic regime.

Without a means of absolute dating, neither Mellars' nor Laville's chronology could be confirmed or refuted. Recent application of thermoluminescence dating to Paleolithic flints may provide a means of correlating Mousterian culture histories. The dates obtained by Valladas *et al.* (1986, 1987) allowed Mellars (1986, 1988) another opportunity to rework Laville's chronology. In the latest scenario, deposits from the sites of Combe Grenal and Le Moustier would seem to be nearly sequential rather than contemporary as argued by Laville. Only MTA industries would overlap and Charentian industries would precede the MTA at Combe Grenal. The sequence of Ferrassie, Quina and MTA would not be contradicted by known archaeological sections. Although these dates may turn out to be accurate, problems with thermoluminescence dating in this time range have yet to be resolved (Webb 1988, Jelinek 1990b). Discussion continues on the chronological ordering of Périgordian sites and Mousterian assemblages, but no resolution is possible without more accurate dating techniques.

Functional Variation
Although first developed by Leslie Freeman (1964, 1966), the functional explanation for variability of Mousterian industrial types is most closely associated with Lewis Binford. Binford and his wife Sally used factor analysis to discern covariance of tool types that might crosscut Bordes' industrial groupings (1966, 1969). The assemblages that they used came from two Southwest Asian and one French site. Each of these lithic collections exhibited high indices of Levallois technique. Analysis of the assemblages indicated five sets of tool groups that closely paralleled Bordes' groups. Like Freeman, the Binfords felt that these "factors" represented functional groups of tools or "tool kits." Although none of the assemblages was

classified as Quina Mousterian due to high Levallois indices, the Binfords found two factors that aligned with Ferrassie. Two of the factors indicated maintenance activities (Factor I-Typical; Factor III-MTA) while the other three assemblage groups represented debris from specific extractive tasks. Denticulate assemblages (Factor IV) were considered to show evidence of plant processing, while Ferrassie assemblages (Factors II & V) reflected hunting and butchering activities. The Binford's multivariate analysis suggested an opposition of even and serrated edged tools which they interpreted as evidence of different activities and their respective tool requirements.

The Binford's analyses are not considered to be a valid test of Bordes' hypotheses on Middle Paleolithic variability. First, only Mousterian industries of Levallois facies were analyzed. Second, the French data was taken from an open-air quarry station, hardly comparable to stratified rockshelter deposits. Jelinek (1976) has also pointed out that the Binfords' factors crosscut Bordes' traditions, and their opposing interpretations of variability are therefore not mutually exclusive. Finally, the problems of sample size and pattern recognition in factor analysis as used by the Binfords have been noted by Cowgill (1968). These vulnerabilities in the Binfords' methodology have left their conclusions open to serious scrutiny, helping to stimulate research along new lines of investigation.

New Directions: Edge Morphology
One of the most significant new directions in Middle Paleolithic lithic analysis was first explored by Nicholas Rolland. Rolland (1977, 1981, 1988a) began his investigations of Middle Paleolithic variability using Bordes tool types and industrial variants but discerned broader axes of variation during the course of his studies. Working with tool frequencies from 120 Mousterian assemblages, Rolland found that these frequencies were continuous and unimodal. These numbers suggested that tool morphology reflected a single phenomenon rather than several distinct traditions. The analysis also suggested that high implement frequencies were most dependent on increased frequencies of scrapers. Rolland's data suggested that higher frequencies of unretouched flakes in assemblages with few scrapers appear to have functionally replaced the smooth, even edged tools found in scraper rich assemblages. Implement frequencies also indicated to Rolland that the Typical and MTA assemblages were more closely aligned with denticulate-rich industries than with the scraper-rich Charentian industries.

Rolland's hypothesis that implement frequencies, specifically scraper frequencies, were unimodal for a large number of Middle Paleolithic collections implied that Bordes' typology of tools was redundant. To determine the role of morphological instability in Mousterian assemblages, Dibble (1984, 1987a, 1988, 1989) examined the intensity of retouch and size of scrapers from several Middle Paleolithic sites. He suggested that Bordes' scraper classes (types 9 - 29) might represent stages in a reduction sequence rather than distinct tool forms. Distinguishing tool classes by the shape and intensity of edge reduction, Bordes recognized the importance of working edges to tools, yet he classified them into discrete groups. Dibble found that two patterns of reduction could account for most of the variability in known Mousterian scraper forms. A flake could be transformed by continuous modification on two edges (single > double > convergent) or one edge (single > transverse). The choice of reduction sequence seemed to be highly correlated with the technology of blank production. Levallois flakes tended to be reduced on two sides rather than one; Dibble inferred that the elongated shape of Levallois flakes was more suitable to such reduction. Thicker flakes and short-wide flakes produced by disc-core and other techniques tended to be reduced on only one edge.

Barton (1988, 1989) has also shown that variability in edge morphology is more continuous than discrete. Working with artifacts from Middle Paleolithic excavations in Spain, he found that several edge attributes, such as edge angle and shape, varied continuously and normally. Building upon Rolland's work with frequencies of unretouched artifacts (1981, 1988a), Barton showed that edges of unretouched or marginally retouched pieces form part of the same continuous distribution as retouched pieces. Barton replicated Dibble's (1987a) findings that tool use and degree of reduction were ultimately controlled by size limitations, particularly flake thickness and width.

Although Barton found that most attributes of edge morphology varied continuously, edge shape did not. Notched pieces seemed to represent a different and distinct type of edge form. Barton described the difference in morphology and intensity of retouch as concentrated on notched pieces, and as laterally extensive on scrapers. Rolland (1981), Dibble (1988) and Jelinek (1988a) have all also proposed that a duality exists between artifacts with notched and even edges. Holdoway *et al.* (n.d.) have demonstrated that denticulates and notched pieces belong to a second, distinct reduction sequence where multiple notches are produced in resharpening. Repeated notching events were found to be correlated with tool length where longer artifacts exhibited more notches. Dibble *et al.* (1995) found no overall size differences in notched tools at Combe-Capelle Bas. However, the site sits on a source of flint. Still, notches in denticulates are smaller there and do appear to represent intensity of use, rather than a distinctive use for the two notched tool types.

These studies suggest that a considerable amount of variability in Mousterian assemblages is related to edge form and reduction intensity. Dibble examined the relative importance of even and serrated edged tools in a number of Mousterian assemblages. He found that "over 90% of interassemblage variability is due to different frequencies of scrapers versus notches and denticulates" (1988:183). This dichotomy also explains a large percentage of the variability between Mousterian industrial variants (over 80% according to Dibble). Examination of the frequencies of tool classes other than scrapers or denticulate/notched relative only to themselves, Dibble found that although bifaces have been used to distinguish MTA assemblages, variation in biface frequencies does not seem to be statistically significant. Bifaces occur in varying frequencies independent of other tool classes. Excluding bifaces from the typological classification of such industries would align MTA-A with Typical Mousterian

industries and MTA-B with Denticulate Mousterian, a suggestion advanced by Bordes many years ago (1953).

In a similar vein, Jelinek (1988a) analyzed intensity of retouch in a number of French Mousterian assemblages. Jelinek's analysis also suggests that tool frequencies and reduction intensity in MTA-A assemblages are most similar to Typical Mousterian while MTA-B assemblages are most like Denticulate industries. Bifaces tended to occur with assemblages that do not have high numbers of tools with continuously modified edges. These data indicate that bifacially flaked tools may also replace scrapers in assemblages with few even edged tools. Analysis of tool assemblages from excavations at Tabun show a cyclical pattern in the proportion of even edged tools (Jelinek 1982a). Bifaces and scrapers alternate in prominence throughout the archaeological sequence and Jelinek suggests a possible environmental correlation with these cultural cycles.

New Directions: Raw Material

Although recent analysis related to tool edge morphology appears to account for much of Mousterian lithic variability, the cause or causes of such variation have not been demonstrated. Variability in the production of tools with even or serrated edges may be related to functional or environmental differences. Intensity and mode of reduction in Mousterian lithic assemblages have also been related to the availability of raw material.

In his study of Mousterian debitage from three French and two Israeli sites, Fish (1979, 1981) found that flake size was highly correlated with raw material availability. At Qafzeh, Tabun, and Corbiac where large flint nodules were readily available, the flakes were wider and longer than at Pech de l'Azé and Combe Grenal. Because the sites with larger flakes also have twice the frequency of Levallois artifacts, Fish suggests that overall presence of this reduction technique correlates with the size and availability of flint nodules. In the Levant where flint is relatively easily acquired, Levallois production is consistently high. Open air sites on the flint rich plateaus of northern France also tend to have high Levallois components (Rolland and Dibble 1990). In contrast, heavily occupied shelters of southwest France tend to have lower indices of Levallois over time. If Levallois technology is associated with readily available flint, then intensive use of local resources may be a cause for decreased Levallois indices. Diminished availability of raw material may help to explain Mellars (1969) findings that Quina industries with low Levallois indices tend to occur over Ferrassie industries within the same site.

Dibble (1985) also examined the relationship between flake size and raw material availability. Dibble, and Jelinek and Dibble on separate occasions, recorded the length, width, and thickness of flakes from 17 French Mousterian assemblages. In order to control for metric differences due to technique of reduction, only Levallois flakes were selected for inclusion in Dibble's study. He found that little or none of the variation in flake size could be associated with differences in Mousterian industrial type. Flakes from different assemblages grouped together by site despite technological differences between assemblages within a site.

Kuhn's (1990, 1991) analyses of lithics from Mousterian strata at two Italian sites suggest that raw material availability is particularly linked to core reduction. Assemblages from the site with immediate access to flint pebbles have many more casual cores that assemblages from the site where raw material is not present. However, raw material availability did not effect the intensity of tool reduction. Kuhn ties some of the variation in tool reduction in the Italian assemblages to differential transport. He suggests that the reduction of cores is linked to geographical characteristics, while reduction of tools is more closely related to functional requirements.

Analysis of the lithic assemblages from several Middle Paleolithic sites within the Avdat/Aqev area of the Central Negev have also shown that lithic reduction and access to raw material may be related. Munday (1976, 1979) and Marks (1983, 1989) have both suggested that interrelated patterns of lithic reduction and subsistence acquisition can be tied to environmental fluctuations. During the analysis of lithic material from two stratified and nine surface sites in the Negev, Munday (1976) found that debitage size and core weight were strongly correlated with distance of transport. Lithic artifacts found farther from available flint showed greater preparation and reduction. Munday (1979) posited that during periods of greater aridity occupants of the Negev were more mobile than during cooler, moister stadial conditions. In an arid environment with low productivity, cores seemed to be radially prepared and the resulting debitage was broader. With decreased pressure on resources during more advantageous climatic conditions, core preparation seems to have been more intensive resulting in more elongated flakes. Marks (1989) felt that this shift in technology was an adaptive change that was secondarily reflected in shifting settlement patterns.

The effect of the environment on Mousterian assemblage variability has also been considered by Rolland (1981). Correlation with environmental data showed that scraper-rich assemblages, especially Quina Mousterian, were most often associated with severe cold regimes while MTA and Denticulate industries were most often found under more temperate conditions. Rolland suggested that perhaps Bordes' Mousterian variants reflected states of transformation of the same industrial complex. Scraper-rich industries could be the result of periods of limited mobility under severe environmental conditions where raw material was intensively utilized. At the other end of the spectrum, denticulate-rich assemblages could have accumulated under less rigorous conditions where higher mobility allowed greater access to quarries. Artifacts with serrated edges have been related in ethnographic studies (Bordes 1962; Leroi-Gourhan 1956) to activities involving plant materials, and thus correlation with temperate conditions could be appropriate. Although Rolland's (1981) correlation of Denticulate industries with milder climatic regimes holds true for a majority of cases, these assemblages are also infrequently associated with more severe climates. A small percentage of scraper-rich Charentian assemblages are also recovered in contexts of relatively moderate climatic conditions.

Rolland and Dibble (1990) have found other evidence of climatic influence upon Mousterian industrial variation. Not only did scraper rich industries tend to be associated with cold and dry paleoclimates in Western Europe in their analyses, but assemblages with heavily reduced scrapers tended to be found in enclosed sites. In other areas, such as the Levant, Rolland and Dibble suggest that assemblages with intensively reduced tools (i.e. Yabrudian) were most often produced during dry phases when resources there were less predictable. Unfortunately, limited archaeological collections and tenuous climatic and chronological correlations for the Levant make these broad associations set forth by Dibble and Rolland difficult to prove. Dibble and Rolland (1990) have suggested that intensive occupation in frigid Europe was mandated by an "aggregated resource pattern" while higher mobility during less severe climate took advantage of a more locally "dispersed resource pattern".

Geneste (1985, 1989, 1990a, 1990b), Turq (1987), Meignen (1988), and Jelinek (1991) have related reduction strategies, raw material, and mobility in the French Middle Paleolithic. By sourcing raw material from archaeological sites, these studies have associated lithic by-products with reduction sequences within a spatial framework. Geneste, a pioneer in flint sourcing and analysis, grouped the lithics from several Middle Paleolithic sites in the Périgord into sequential stages of manufacture. He then correlated the products of each reduction phase with raw material type to compare intra- and inter-site patterns of mobility and procurement. Since flint sources can be "finger printed", Geneste's work has a fairly high degree of resolution. Proportions of six primary raw material types remained relatively stable for each locus throughout the Middle Paleolithic and into the Upper Paleolithic. The majority of raw material (88 per cent on average) came from within five kilometers of a site, 2 to 20 per cent came from a distance of 5 to 20 kilometers, while resources between 30 to 80 kilometers were only sporadically used. As in Munday's (1979) study, materials from greater distances were consistently more reduced before arrival at their depositional context than materials recovered nearby.

Using Geneste's (1985) data, Jelinek (1991) looked at the relationship between raw material type and reduction technique. He found that the most abundant material at each site was used in the production of a high proportion of cortical flakes and non-specialized debitage. The second most abundant material seems to have been used for more patterned sequences of production (i.e. Levallois) and in a higher proportion of retouched artifacts. This selection can be tied to earlier findings by Fish (1979) on the economy of flint and Levallois production.

Analysis of lithics from the site of La Borde, south of the Dordogne Valley along the Lot River, revealed two patterns of lithic provision (Turq 1987). Local quartz comprised most of the assemblage, but only 5 per cent of these flakes had been retouched into tools. Reduction of exotic flint reflected very different technological patterns. Only 3 per cent of the total assemblage was made out of flint, but a full third of the flint at La Borde had been retouched into tools.

Meignen (1988; Meignen and Vandermeersch 1986) analyzed the lithics from several Quina Mousterian assemblages at the site of Marillac also in the Charente. She found that local and non-local flint were being used in very different ways. Material available locally was not intensively reduced. Many of the recovered artifacts made of local flint were cortical flakes, unretouched flakes and denticulate tools. In contrast, the artifacts of non-local flint consisted primarily of scrapers and small, short-wide flakes. The scrapers tended to be large and thick, while the flakes of exotic material were smaller than flakes of local material. Meignen interpreted these small exotic flakes with exterior scalar retouch as evidence of scraper edge rejuvenation. She suggested that tools with even edges were prepared elsewhere and transported to the site, while denticulates were made expediently out of locally available flint.

Conclusion

The study of Mousterian lithic assemblages began with description and classification. The typology developed by François Bordes helped to guide this process and subsequent analysis. Bordes enabled archaeologists to quantitatively compare entire lithic assemblages rather than merely rely upon the presence or absence of certain tool types for comparability. His analyses showed that much lithic variation could be accounted for by grouping sets of tools into Mousterian variants. Although these variants were repeatedly recognized at Middle Paleolithic sites, no explanation for their occurrence was ever found. The continuing emphasis on retouched tools and their invariant cultural expression can be traced from the *fossil directeur* approach of the early twentieth century. This organic view of cultural development has strongly influenced Paleolithic analyses throughout most of this century.

Recent studies of Middle Paleolithic assemblages suggest that intensity of tool reduction can account for a great deal of variability in Mousterian tool morphology. Retouched tools may be more productively viewed as parts of reduction continua rather than discrete, individual types. Even and serrated edged tools appear to vary independently from one another. Variation in core manufacture and reduction have been shown to vary in relation to raw material availability. These changes in lithic production and/or intensity of use may be viewed as adaptations or reactions to external stress, particularly environmental stress. As suggested by Kuhn (1991) and Dibble (1995), changes in core reduction, tool production, and tool reduction all appear to be tied to access to raw material, but each of these aspects of lithic technology seems to vary independently of the others.

This analysis of the lithic from La Quina was designed to test these concepts of hunter-gatherer raw material use. Traditional typological classification was recorded, but this data is also compared with the rest of the lithic assemblage. Attributes to discern variation in tool morphology, reduction technique, and intensity of reduction between the strata at La Quina were recorded in this analysis. This variation will be compared to climatological evidence from the site to discern changes in economy and settlement in the Middle Paleolithic.

CHAPTER III

LA QUINA: THE SITE

The Paleolithic site of La Quina was discovered in 1872. In the past century, three excavation teams have investigated the archaeological remains at the site. These investigations have been led by Dr. Henri-Martin, by his daughter Germaine Henri-Martin, and most recently by Arthur Jelinek and André Debénath. The history of each of these excavations is examined in this chapter. Archaeological evidence for geological and environmental change has been correlated with cultural remains to reconstruct prehistoric site use as it has been understood by each investigative team.

Geographical Position

The site of La Quina lies at the southeastern extreme of the Charente region of Southwest France (Fig. 1). At present, the department of the Charente is characterized by low rolling hills and small stream valleys. The topography is the result of repeated episodes of vigorous fluvial action on a limestone plateau. Water and frost action have carved cliffs and rock shelters in the walls of a number of Charentian valleys. Cultural remains of various Paleolithic periods extend for nearly a kilometer along the southeastern edge of the Voultron River valley at the site of La Quina (Fig. 2). The Voultron is a distant tributary of the Dordogne River in the French Périgord region. The Périgord has a topography similar to the Charente, but its valleys are more deeply incised and its plateaus less eroded. The karstic system of caves and the numerous rock shelters along river valleys in the Périgord contain many stratified Paleolithic sites. For this reason, the Dordogne drainage basin has been extensively and intensively studied by prehistorians. In fact, the area has served as a frame of reference for Middle and Upper Paleolithic research in Western Europe. Although the archaeological remains of the Charente region are less well known than those of the Périgord proper, they clearly represent an extension of the same Paleolithic cultural traditions.

Within the deposits at La Quina, two relatively distinct cultural concentrations have been recognized (Fig. 3). These areas were designated the "Station Amont" and the "Station Aval" by Dr. Henri-Martin (1909). The Station Amont includes deposits at the middle to northeastern end of the site and is predominantly Middle Paleolithic in content. These cultural remains once stretched almost 100 meters along the river valley, but only a small portion (nine meters) of the station remains today (D in Fig. 3). The sediments form a triangular wedge more than 7 meters high and extending to a maximum of 15 meters from the cliff face. The Station Amont is noted for its dense concentration of animal bone and large quantities of Mousterian lithics. Deposits at the Station Amont have been the focus of all three investigations. Recent excavations by Debénath and Jelinek have been limited to this area.

The Station Aval lies at the southwestern end of the La Quina deposits 200 meters from the Station Amont. This area seems to have been used later in time and less intensively. Late Mousterian, Chatelperronian and Aurignacian remains, including a series of hearths, were discovered under extensive

limestone collapse by Dr. Henri-Martin.

History of Excavation

The presence of cultural materials at La Quina was first recognized by Gustave Chauvet in 1872. He described Mousterian and Magdalenian industries along the cliffs of the Voultron valley as part of a regional surface survey (Chauvet 1896, 1897). The archaeological significance of the site was revealed in 1881 during road construction. A route along the edge of the Voultron flood plain grazed the base of the cultural strata. The talus that was used as ballast contained shaped flints and broken animal bone. At this time the density of the archaeological material was recognized, although locals did not understand its antiquity. Chauvet followed the crew as they leveled the road bed and was able to discern and describe the two distinct cultural areas or "stations" (Henri-Martin 1907).

DR. HENRI-MARTIN

Chauvet and others continued to explore the deposits at La Quina, but Dr. Henri-Martin was the first to mount extensive excavations there. In 1905 he visited the site and became interested in describing the stratigraphy as well as in saving the site from random collection. Dr. Henri-Martin began his venture by buying the land under the site and a nearby farmhouse to serve as home and laboratory. From 1906 to his death in 1936, he conducted systematic excavations in wide trenches perpendicular to the cliff face at La Quina. Although Dr. Henri-Martin put in more than 20 test trenches along the southeast wall of the Voultron Valley, he concentrated his excavations at the Station Amont (Fig. 3). Here he excavated eight trenches, three of which conjoined to form a 35 m wide swath from the cliff face to the road (Fig. 3: A - C). He also fully excavated areas P, M, G and Z. Dr. Henri-Martin noted continuity in origin for the sedimentological layers the length of the Station Amont with slight variation in geological and cultural detail between each exposure.

Stratigraphy

The profile that most closely approximates the recent excavations in the remaining nine-meter section (Fig 3: D) of the Station Amont is Dr. Henri-Martin's drawing of trench C (1923b:33)(Fig. 4). In this section, he described a large cone of limestone talus piled against the cliff face. The weathering of frost-cracked limestone (*éboulis*) created an overhang of 1.5 meters at the top of the section. The basal stratum, Bed 5, was comprised of sand and rounded limestone fragments that were tinged red from iron salts. This layer was capped by a bed of sand with the earliest Mousterian artifacts (Bed 4). Differences in patination suggested to Dr. Henri-Martin that these early lithics represented industries of various ages. The few recovered tools were unifacially flaked and highly variable in morphology. Bed 4 was also described as containing large quantities of reindeer bone and antler.

Bed 3, a stratified yellow-green clayey sand, also contained lithic material. Dr. Henri-Martin described these artifacts as a "median Mousterian" industry, intermediate in technology

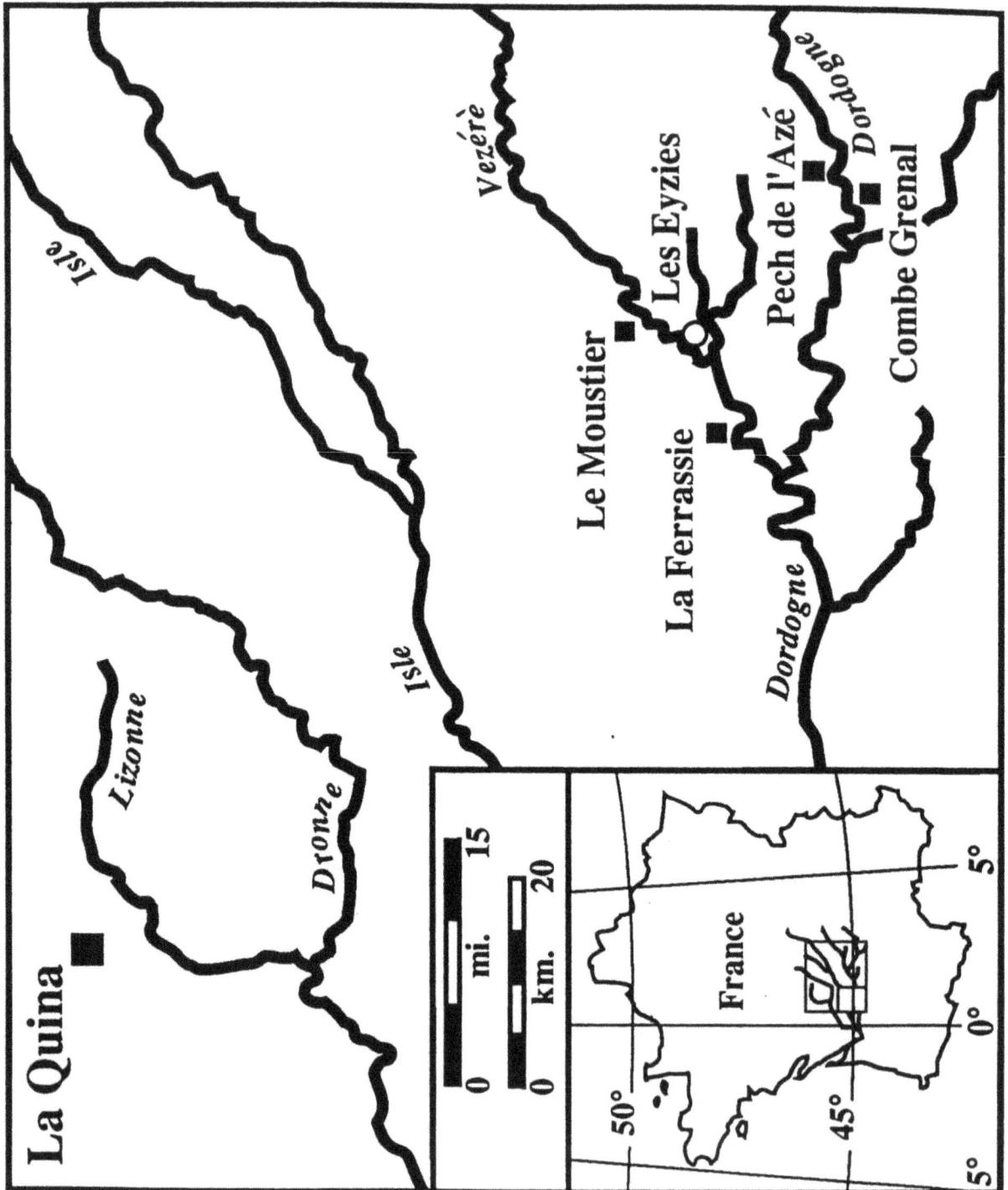

Figure 1. Map of France and location of La Quina (O'Brien)

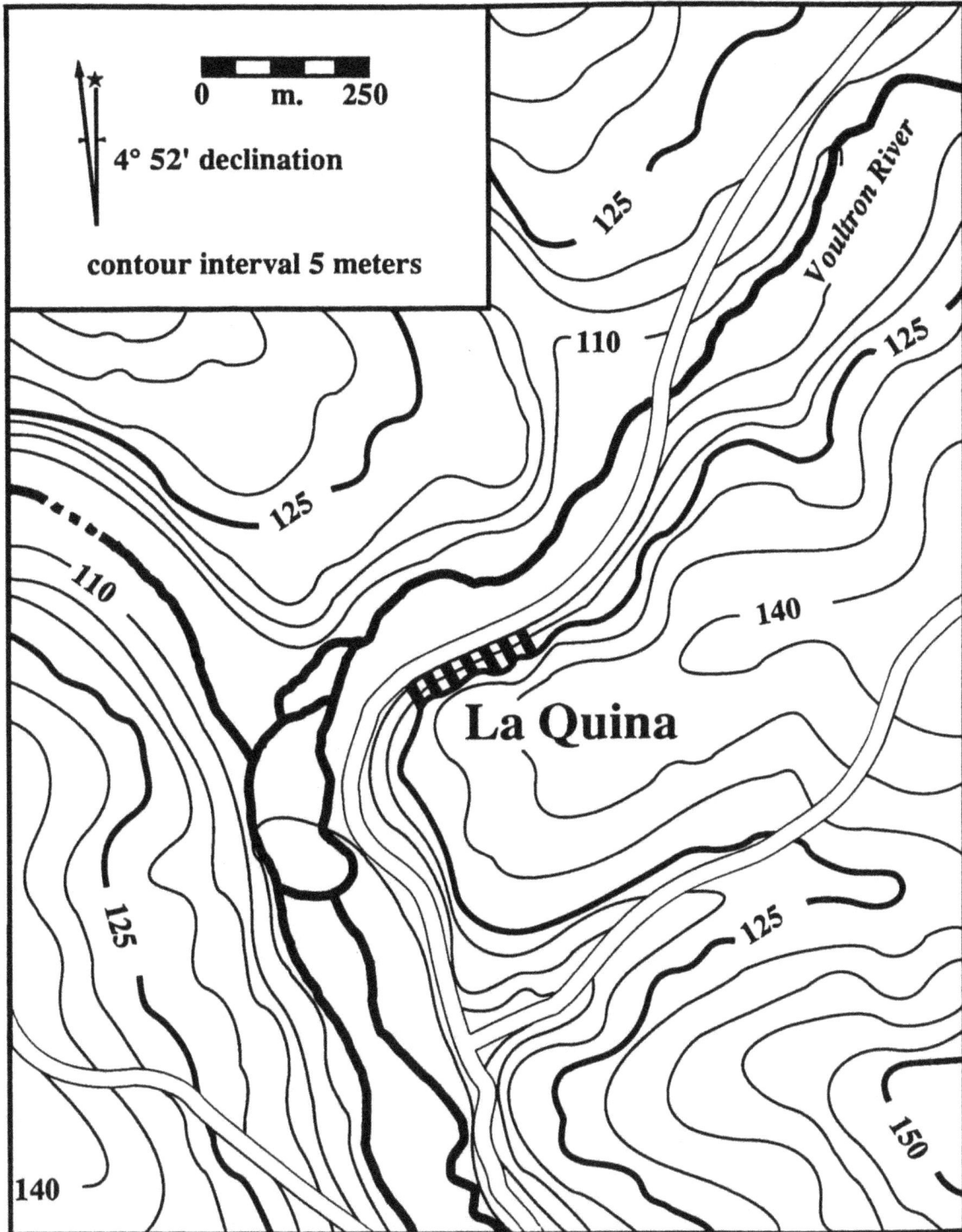

Figure 2. Contour map of Voultron Valley (O'Brien)

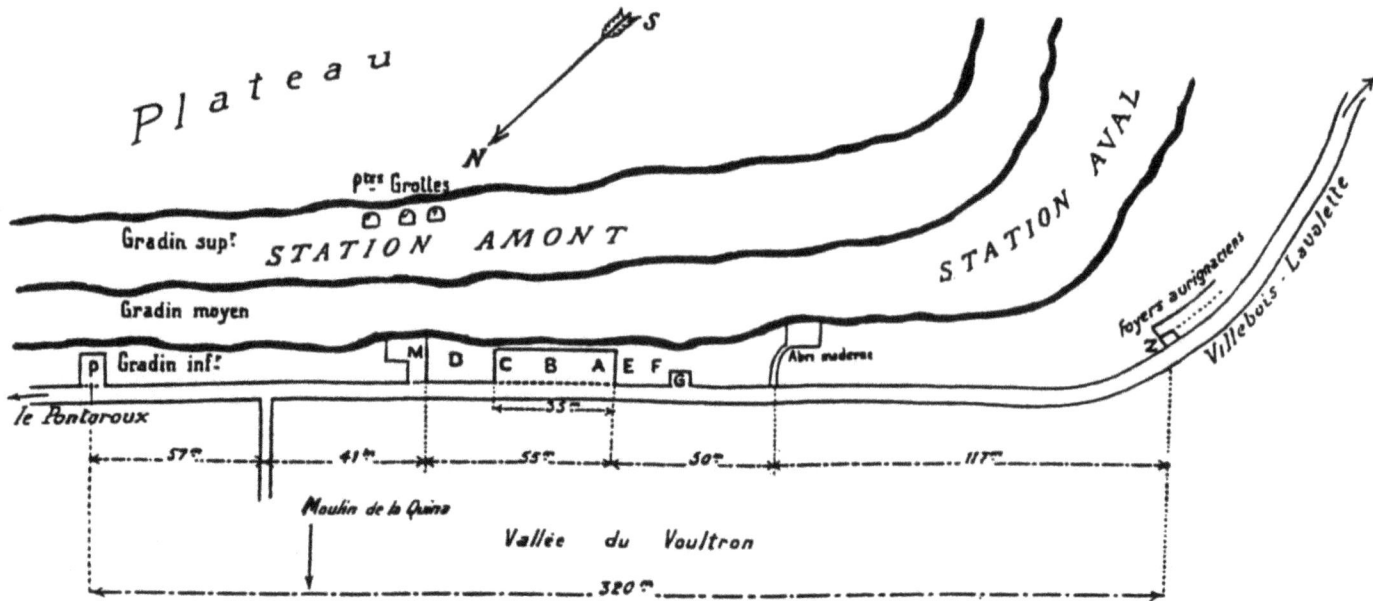

Figure 3. Plan of La Quina - current excavations in "D" (Henri-Martin 1923b:13)

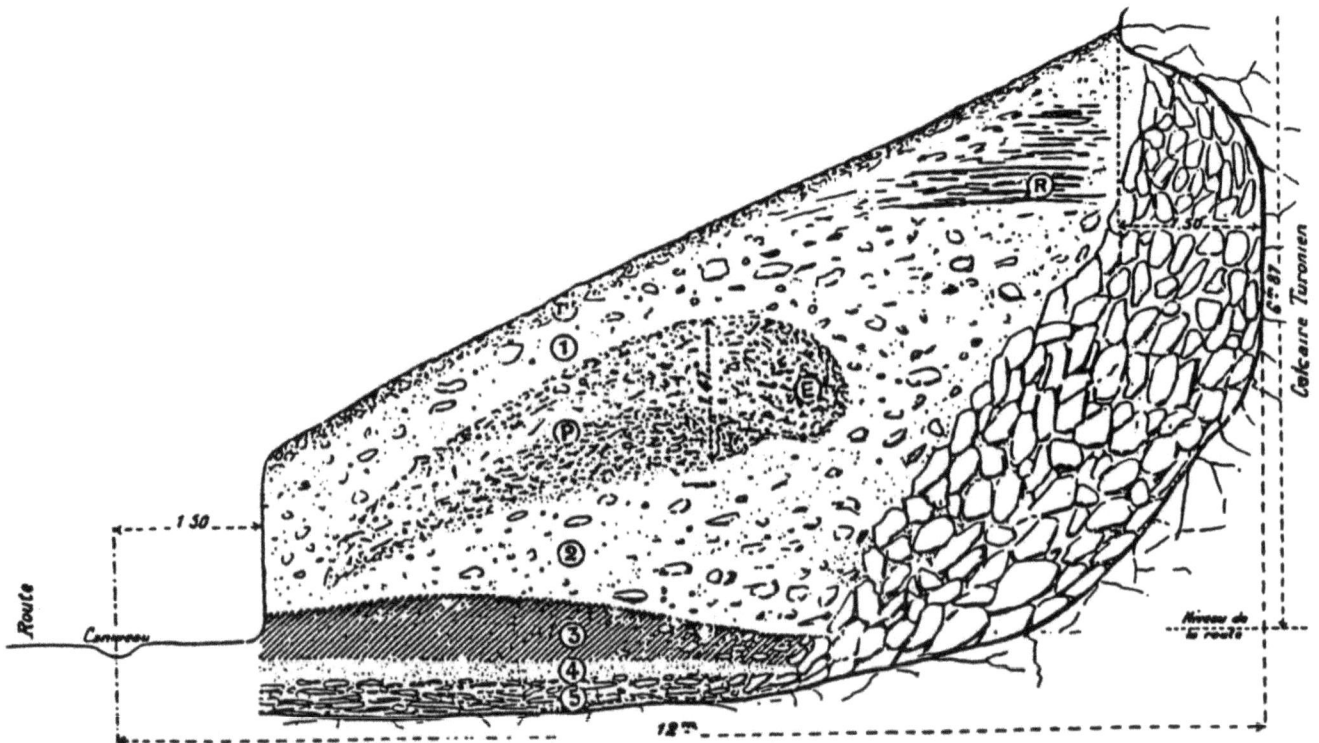

Figure 4. Profile at Trench C (Henri-Martin 1923b:33)

between the preceding and subsequent lithic assemblages. Bed 3 formed the top of the horizontal basal strata at La Quina. The faunal assemblage for this level was comprised of reindeer, horse, and bovids. A smaller number of bones of wolf, fox, hyena, mammoth, birds and rodents were also recovered. The abundance of animal bone found in this level suggested to Dr. Henri-Martin that unusable cultural material was being discarded from above, from habitations on the cliff terraces. A female Neanderthal skeleton (H5) was found in the lower portion of Bed 3 to the southwest of the remaining section. This lithic assemblage was described as having more even retouch with more regularity and variety in form than the earliest Mousterian artifacts. Dr. Henri-Martin found numbers of bifacial choppers, triangular points, scrapers, and limestone spheres.

Dr. Henri-Martin felt that the lithics in Beds 1 and 2 had evolved to a "perfected" Mousterian industry. Beds 1 and 2 were the first to slope from the cliff face toward the river valley. The beds were comprised of a mixture of sand, limestone fragments, and cultural material. In the middle of this thick unit he described a concentration of lithics, burned and utilized bone (P in Fig. 4). A Neanderthal child's skull (H 18) was found in this "pocket". Dr. Henri-Martin believed these sediments had also come down from occupations on the upper terraces. The lithic assemblage was characterized by quantities of intensively retouched scrapers and points with alternate marginal retouch on the interior surface.

Although the lower and middle layers at La Quina are generally similar in each of Dr. Henri-Martin's exposures along the length of the Station Amont, the upper beds show more lateral variation. At the top of the sequence in trench C, Dr. Henri-Martin found a meter of what he described as horizontal hearths (R in Fig. 4). The unusual deposits were very rich in burned bone but lithic artifacts were relatively rare. Finally, the entire slope of deposit was capped by a layer of historic organic material (Henri-Martin 1923b).

Cultural Analysis
Dr. Henri-Martin described a sequence of production and reduction of the stone artifacts at La Quina. He theorized that the tools were made on local flint with quartz pebbles or shaped bone used for percussion. Although he never found a flint source at the site, Dr. Henri-Martin thought that several localities of different flint must have been accessible to the occupants of La Quina (1923a).

Analysis of chipped stone tools from La Quina suggested an evolution in morphology and technology to Dr. Henri-Martin. The basal units at La Quina contained a less abundant and less "perfected" lithic industry. Stone tools were patinated to varying degrees, showed no consistency in form, and were only unifacially retouched. In the middle strata, Dr. Henri-Martin found numerous scrapers, those later known as Quina scrapers. The intensive retouch on these convex-edged tools suggested to him that they had blunted quickly in use and had been resharpened frequently. Tool form showed more regularity and more variation than in the basal levels. Dr. Henri-Martin felt that the "most perfected" Mousterian industry was recovered

from the top of the middle layers, his Beds 1 and 2 (1936). Although Dr. Henri-Martin recovered bifacially worked tools at La Quina, he never explicitly treated the evolution of this technology.

In the first five years of excavation, Dr. Henri-Martin found only a few loose human bones; two astragali, a cranial fragment, a vertebra, and two teeth. Disappointed but undaunted, he began to study the multitude of animal bones recovered from La Quina. He examined and experimented with butchering techniques to try to understand the markings, perforations, and abrasions on the Quina faunal remains. Dr. Henri-Martin felt that the damage on the large bovid, horse, and reindeer bones was due to Neanderthal butchery and subsequent utilization (1907, 1909). The cut marks exhibited regularity in placement indicating patterns of disarticulation, skinning, and fleshing. The bones were also regularly broken for extraction of marrow and for use as tools. The distal portion of bovid humeri had frequently been shaped for use in knapping. Other bones and bone splinters also showed wear characteristic of lithic manufacture. Dr. Henri-Martin believed that every part of the carcass was used by the inhabitants of La Quina; the meat, the hide, the organs, and the bones (1923a).

The human remains from La Quina represent the most important collection of Neanderthals in the region. In 1911, Dr. Henri-Martin found the remains of a nearly complete skeleton. Over the next two and a half decades, he recovered parts of at least 21 additional individuals (Vandermeersch 1976). Hominid 5, also known as the "woman of La Quina", was excavated from muddy basal sediments of the ancient Voultron stream. The discovery of the cranium, vertebrae, femora and humeri of the 25 year-old female came shortly after the discovery of Neanderthal remains at La Chapelle-aux-Saints, Le Moustier, and La Ferrassie. The only other complete skull found at La Quina (a child's cranium ± 8 years old) was recovered four years later from Dr. Henri-Martin's "organic pocket" between Beds 1 and 2.

Climatic Reconstruction and Site Use
Dr. Henri-Martin used a combination of geology and faunal analysis to reconstruct climate during the occupation of La Quina. In the deepest layers of the site, the remains of reindeer were predominant. Dr. Henri-Martin recognized this fauna as an indicator of cold climate. Reindeer bones were present throughout the sequence, but bones of bovids and equids became more plentiful in the middle and upper beds. The faunal collections indicated that climate was never temperate during the Mousterian occupation of La Quina, but was somewhat ameliorated in the final stages (1936).

The sediments at La Quina suggested to Dr. Henri-Martin that gradual desiccation had occurred over time. At the base of the section, strong water action had scoured a platform. Then gentler stream flow deposited horizontal layers of sand and clay. He believed that the middle and upper beds were comprised of geological and cultural detritus from the upper terraces that had accumulated as a dry wedge on top of the horizontal strata. The angular and rounded fragments of frost-cracked limestone in the sloping beds reflected relatively cold conditions. Analysis of sediments from La Quina also indicated relatively cold conditions with gradual warming over time.

Dr. Henri-Martin also postulated about the subsistence and lifestyle of the Neanderthals at La Quina. He thought that the sheer size of the animals butchered at La Quina would have posed problems in hunting and transport. The presence of all skeletal elements in the faunal collection indicated that hunting was practiced near the site. Although Dr. Henri-Martin was uncertain as to hunting techniques used by the site occupants, he offered a number of theories. The limestone spheres he found could have been used as bolas, while the recovered flint points could have been used as projectiles. With the discovery of a stone point in the phalanx of a bovid, Dr. Henri-Martin felt confident in assuming that the Neanderthals had hunted with lances. He also hypothesized about the use of traps, lassos and wooden tools that had not preserved but would have facilitated the capture of large game (1936).

La Quina certainly served as a hunting and butchering site, but evidence of habitation was also present. Quantities of burned and unburned bone mixed with products of lithic reduction suggested some periods of occupation in the area. Yet, the orientation of the site is unusual for habitation. Most Paleolithic sites face south to gain solar radiation. La Quina faces to the northwest. Dr. Henri-Martin found no well-defined hearths and little calcined bone in his excavations, although he did find quantities of burned animal remains. He believed that the cultural and geological debris of the middle and upper strata had been washed or fallen down from above. He suggested that the occupants had lived in wood and hide huts on the ledge above the site or that they had made use of several small caves there (Fig. 3). He found small hearths and some cultural remains in these upper shelters. Although some of Dr. Henri-Martin's interpretations can be questioned, his work at La Quina was exemplary for its day.

GERMAINE HENRI-MARTIN

The work of Dr. Henri-Martin continued until his death in 1936. At that time, work at the site ceased until 1953 when his daughter, Germaine Henri-Martin recommenced the excavations. She hoped that the technology available to archaeologists would help to refine the interpretation of cultural occupation at La Quina. The study of sedimentology would help to unravel climatological history, while radiocarbon dating might place site use in absolute time (Henri-Martin 1976). Germaine Henri-Martin continued excavations at both Paleolithic stations, clarifying the stratigraphy at each area. She seems to have been most interested in the late Middle Paleolithic strata at the Station Amont and the transitional deposits leading into the Upper Paleolithic at the Station Aval. At the Mousterian station, she defined and described a sequence of occupation in the uppermost layers that had not been previously recognized.

Stratigraphy

Germaine Henri-Martin's interpretation of Section C (Fig. 5) (1969:91) is even more closely aligned with the provisional modern stratigraphy than Dr. Henri-Martin's. The similarity is due in part to her more meticulous study of the section, but also to changes in the actual deposits along the cliff face as she excavated into the existing profile. In Dr. Henri-Martin's drawing of the profile B (1923:20) the upper half of the deposits was a dense layer of limestone collapse. Ten meters to the northeast in trench C (Fig. 4) he found abundant burned bone with a limited number of lithics. Germaine Henri-Martin's excavations into the C profile further exposed these cultural strata first encountered by her father.

In general, Germaine Henri-Martin's interpretation of the lower and middle beds at Section C was extremely close to her father's. She described Beds 6 and 5 as bedded fluvial sands with occasional animal bone and a pre-Mousterian lithic assemblage. The few lithics in Bed 6 were worn. Germaine Henri-Martin collected over 200 tools with variable morphology and crude unifacial and bifacial retouch. Fauna was also relatively scarce at this depth. Bed 5, a greenish clay layer, was a marker bed extending the length of the site. The lithic assemblage of Bed 5 resembled that of Bed 6 but the faunal assemblage was greater. Germaine Henri-Martin classified the lithics as a very primitive Mousterian or Tayacian industry with Clactonian debitage. Bed 4 was a mixture of sand, clay, limestone pebbles, manganese and iron oxide. A Neanderthal temporal bone was recovered from this bed by Germaine Henri-Martin. Bed 4 contained the oldest reindeer bones and the first evidence of a true Mousterian lithic assemblage. As in Dr. Henri-Martin's description of the medial industry, these tools were more regular in overall form and retouch than those recovered below. Bed 3 represented another fluvial sequence of sand and clay deposits. Beds 3 a and b were bedded fluvial sands overlain by a layer of clay. Above these horizontal basal units was a deposit of sterile sand and limestone blocks (2c) which was especially thick near the cliff face. Beds 2 a and b were mixtures of sand, limestone and small amounts of clay with an "evolved" Mousterian industry.

These lower and middle beds were overlain by a series of beds that Germaine Henri-Martin called the "last Mousterian habitat". Although Dr. Henri-Martin noted an increase in burned bone and suggested the presence of hearths, he did not recognized the full extent and density of the cultural material in these upper beds at the Station Amont. The deposits excavated by his daughter were even more densely anthropogenic in nature. The meter of deposits contained high proportions of flint, burned and unburned bone, sand and limestone fragments. The lithic industry in these uppermost beds was defined by Germaine Henri-Martin as that of Denticulate Mousterian (1969). She obtained a carbon date of 35,250 ± 530BP (GrN2526) on burned bone from this level (G. Henri-Martin 1964).

Cultural and Environmental Reconstruction

Germaine Henri-Martin conducted excavations of the middle strata to test her father's hypothesis that the cultural debris had fallen from the upper terraces. She found the densest evidence of habitation closest to the cliff face. She also recognized hearths, work areas, and articulated bones in these beds. Germaine Henri-Martin thought that these cultural remains reflected primary deposition that had been covered by

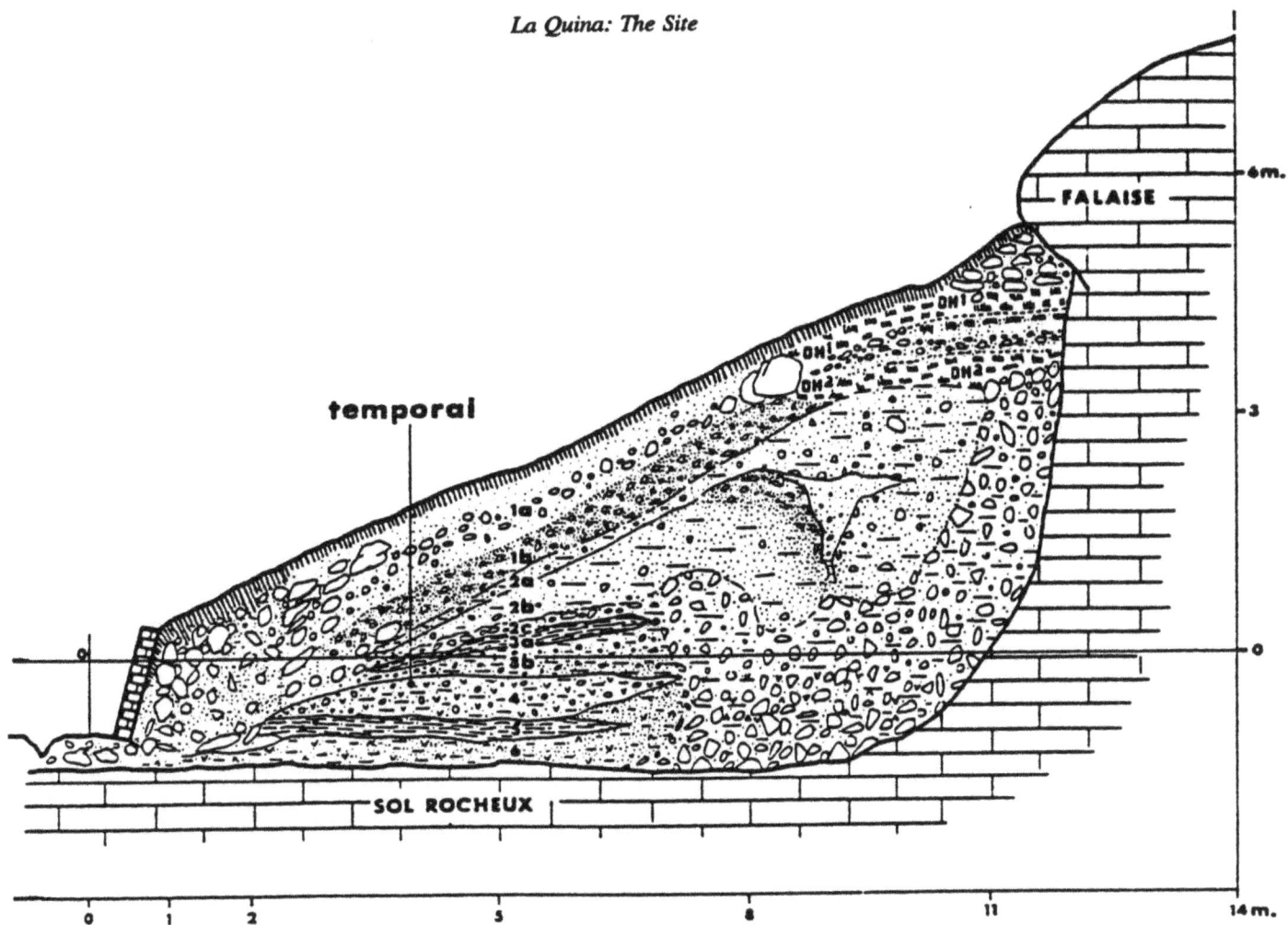

Figure 5. Profile at Trench C (G. Henri-Martin 1969:91)

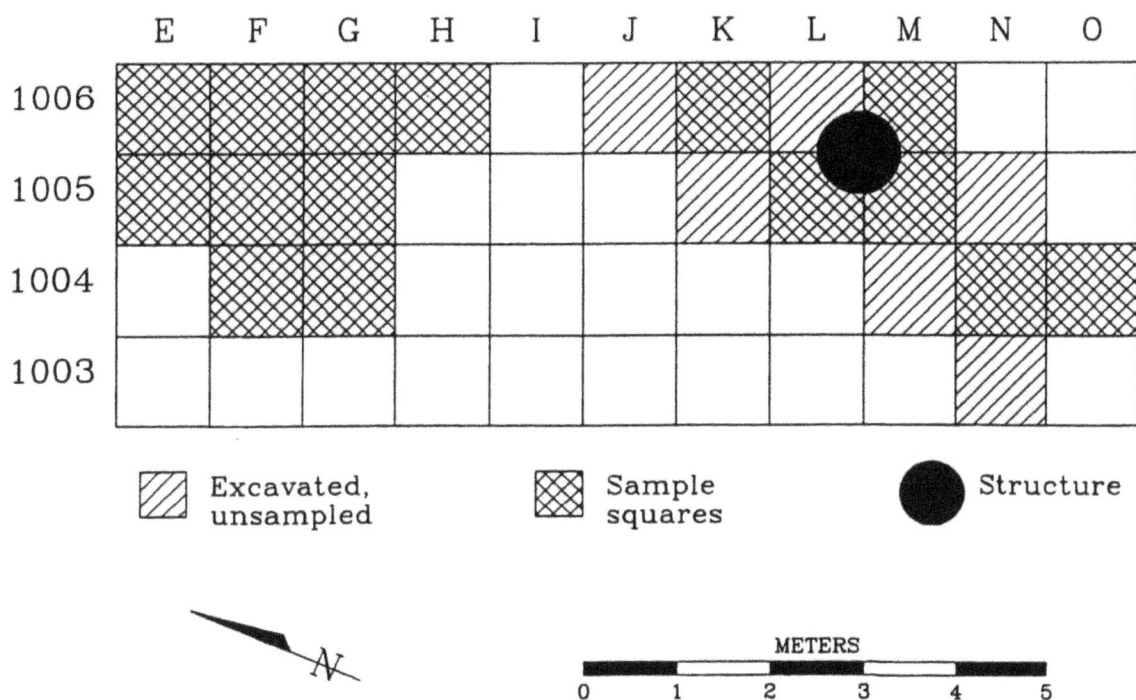

Figure 6. Plan of excavation units: Jelinek/Debenath excavations

subsequent limestone collapse rather than detritus from above. This major limestone collapse preceded the deposition of the upper beds (1976).

Analysis of sediments from La Quina by Henriette Alimen (1951) suggested a chronology similar to that developed by Dr. Henri-Martin. She found evidence of a period of intense cold prior to cultural use of the site. The fluvial nature of the basal sediments reflected an abundance of water and more temperate climate during this period. Alimen envisioned a period of desiccation and intense cold during deposition of the upper slope deposits. This period ended with enormous landslides, possibly caused by earthquakes, followed by a slight rise in temperature. Alimen suggested that the two periods of intense cold related to glacial maxima, while the intervening period of abundant water and sedimentation correlated with an interglacial stage.

Faunal analysis was conducted by Germaine Henri-Martin to examine seasonality in the use of La Quina. She and Yves Guillien (Guillien and Henri-Martin 1974) studied the teeth of sub-adult reindeer excavated from the upper midden strata. They found that all of the deer had been killed during warmer months and were between 1 to 5 months or between 11 to 17 months of age. The animals were killed between birthing and rutting seasons. This evidence suggested repeated use of the site for hunting during warmer months. The absence of reindeer bones from cooler months may reflect seasonal variation in hunting patterns at La Quina. Although doubts about the validity of Guillien's analysis have been raised (Binford 1983), further seasonality studies will be extremely useful for interpreting subsistence patterns and seasonal use of La Quina.

RECENT EXCAVATIONS

Recent excavations at La Quina were begun in 1985 under the direction of Arthur Jelinek (University of Arizona), André Debénath (University of Bordeaux) and Harold Dibble (University of Pennsylvania) at the suggestion of Dr. Henri Delporte of the Musée des Antiquités Nationales at Saint-Germain-en-Laye. The significance of the hominid and cultural remains found in earlier excavations led these researchers to believe that a reevaluation of the site was warranted. The project was designed to test the remaining cultural and geological deposits in a systematic fashion. Although the work of the Henri-Martins was exceptional for its time, no detailed cultural or environmental stratigraphy was ever developed. Excavations continued from 1985 to 1994 were restricted to one face of the remaining nine meter section left between the earlier trenches C and M, and to a deposit of bones left exposed by Germaine Henri-Martin at her death (Fig. 3: primary excavation = D / Bone Bed = A).

By 1991, the time of this analysis, twelve meter-square units had been opened in the upper deposits and five of these units had been fully excavated (Fig. 6). In the middle section of the profile, three half meter-square units were being excavated to clean and straighten the old profile. At the base of the section, six meter-square units had been opened to form a large horizontal expanse, but excavation of these basal deposits had only begun. All of the artifacts recovered from the lower and middle beds between 1985 and 1990 were included in this study. A sample of the excavated material recovered during this time from the upper beds was analyzed in detail. In addition, salvage excavations were conducted on the exposed bone concentration that had been left by Germaine Henri-Martin at the southwest end of the Station Amont. Although stratigraphic association suggests that these deposits were part of Dr. Henri-Martin's layer 2 and Germaine Henri-Martin's layer 2b, the lithic artifacts from this non-contiguous lower bone concentration have not been included in this analysis.

Excavation proceeded in halves of meter-square units using preliminary stratigraphic designations. During excavation, small bone splinters were collected separately for each 25 cm area while small flint and stone was gathered from each 50 cm square. Every artifact over 3 cm as well as every identifiable bone was mapped and numbered individually. The remaining sedimentary material was screened by level during the first years of excavations, and samples are currently being saved for eventual wet screening. High numbers of small flakes and microvertebrate remains will eventually be collected in this manner. As a preliminary control for small stone and bone fragments in this study, three 10 cm x 10 cm column samples were collected in levels 5 cm deep from the full sequence of the upper beds. For comparison, four samples of the same size were collected from two of the lower strata.

The automated system for field recording developed by Dibble and his students greatly facilitated the enormous task of excavation at La Quina (Dibble 1987b). An electronic theodolite coupled with an electronic distance meter (EDM) measured the position of each recorded object on the site and calculated the cartesian coordinates of x, y and z for each point. The speed and accuracy of the system are such that several points can be recorded for any object, giving an idea of dip, strike and general form. The coordinates for points on artifacts, rocks, features, and stratigraphy were automatically stored in a small portable computer at the site. The data were then transferred to a larger microcomputer in the laboratory. All further analyses in the fields of faunal identification, zooarchaeology, and lithic studies are being integrated into this single, all-encompassing computerized data base.

Stratigraphy

Recent excavations have clarified the previously described strata at the northeastern face of Dr. Henri-Martin's Trench C.

In 1984, Debénath established a preliminary numbered stratigraphy for the uppermost layers based upon test excavations near the cliff face (Fig. 7)(Debénath and Jelinek 1985). In 1987, he outlined a series of geological units for the lower and middle strata (Fig. 8). The lower units have been given a series of letter designations prior to eventual integration with the upper numerical sequence (Fig. 9)(Debénath and Jelinek 1987, 1990).

The basal deposits at La Quina are comprised of Beds L - Q in

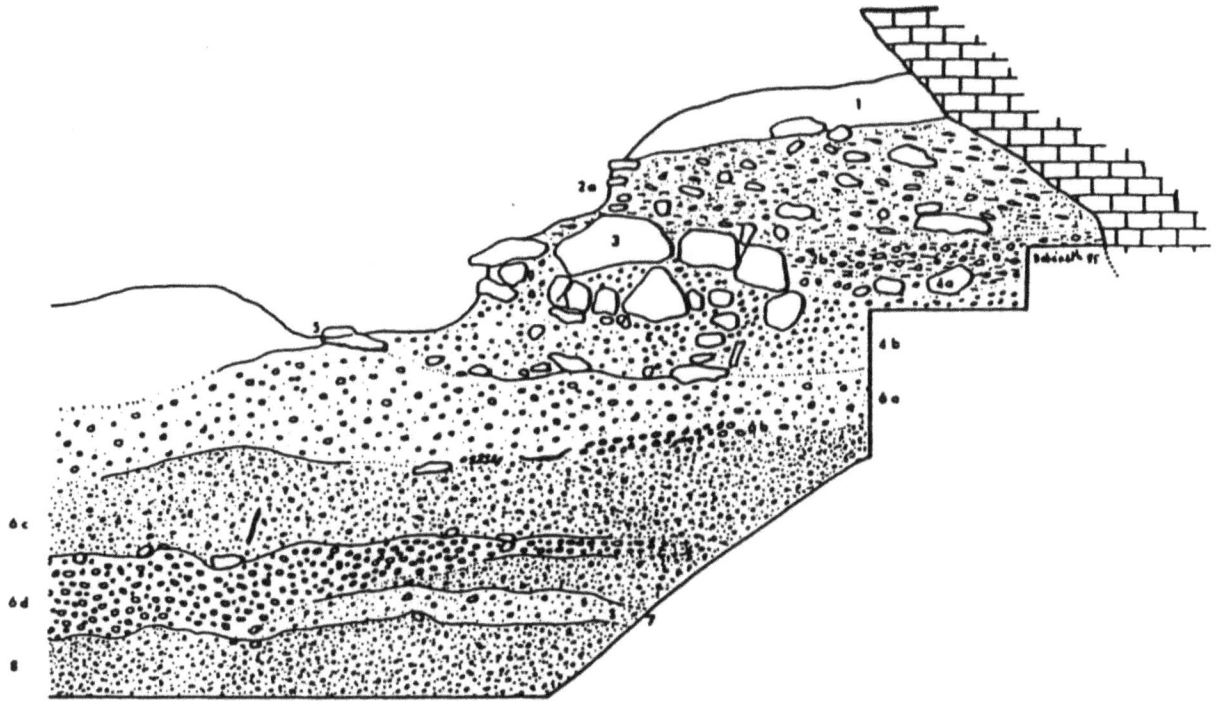

Figure 7. Profile of the upper beds (Debenath 1985)

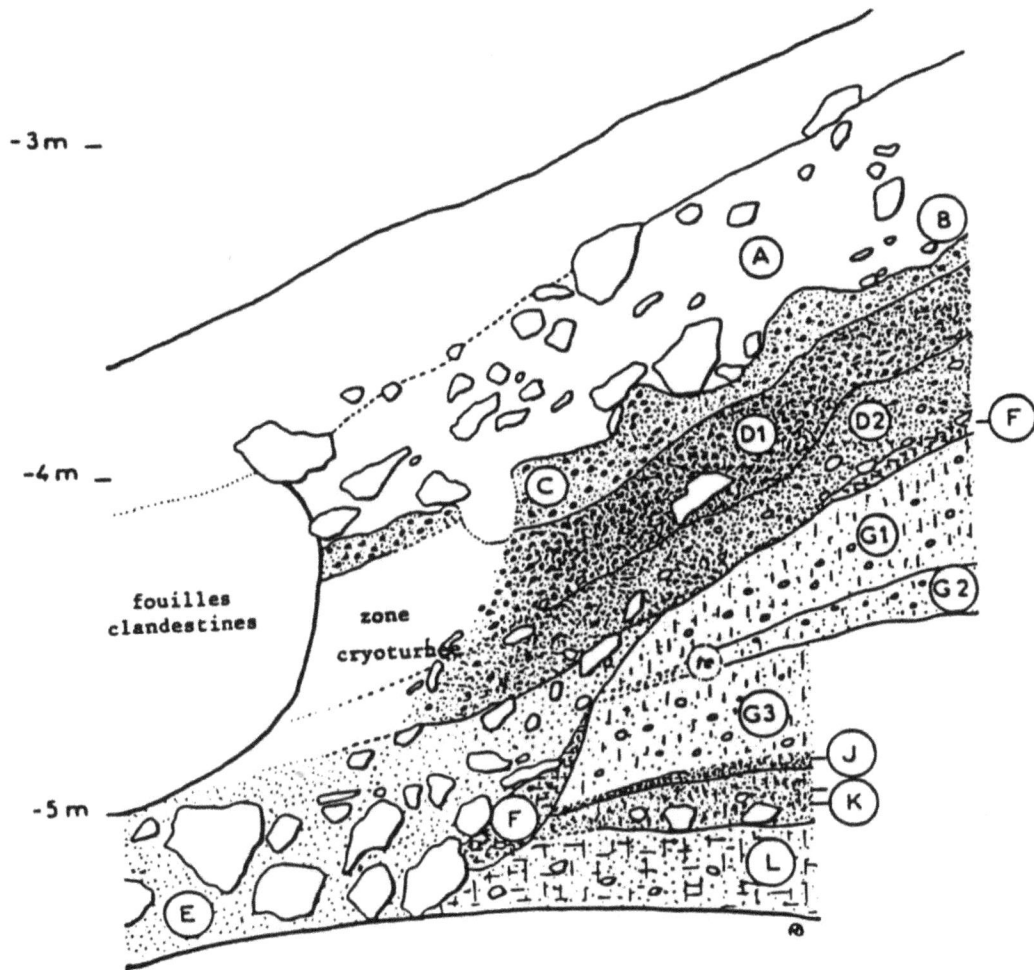

Figure 8. Profile of lower and middle beds (Debenath 1985)

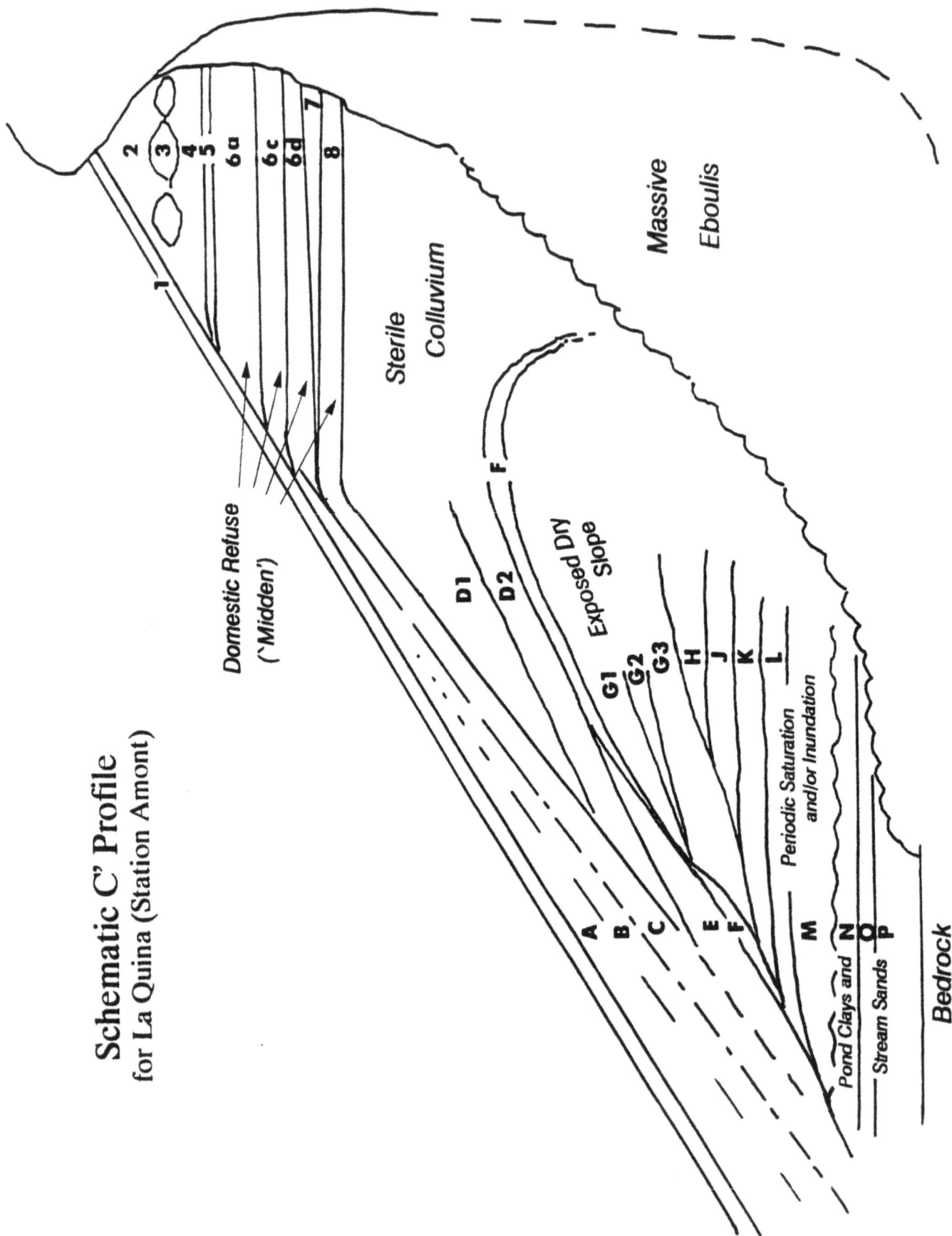

Schematic 'C' Profile
for La Quina (Station Amont)

Domestic Refuse
('Midden')

Sterile
Colluvium

Massive
Eboulis

Exposed Dry
Slope

Periodic Saturation
and/or Inundation

Pond Clays and
Stream Sands

Bedrock

Figure 9. Schematic profile at Trench C (Jelinek n.d.)

Debénath's provisional terminology (Fig. 8). These strata are essentially horizontal and are equivalent to the Henri-Martins' lower strata. A wedge of limestone talus against the cliff face lies between these units and the scarp. The lower beds at La Quina are fluvial in nature, unlike the middle deposits which are comprised of colluvium. As stated previously, a horizontal exposure of approximately 6 meters square had been obtained for these strata by 1990. Although recent excavation has been extremely limited in these beds, preliminary examination suggests that Bed Q - L correspond to Germaine Henri-Martin's Beds 6 - 3.

The basal unit in the sequence, Bed Q, is a series of fine pale yellow/brown fluvial sands. Above this is a deposit of fine greenish clays called Bed P by Debénath and Layer 5 by Germaine Henri-Martin. Bed O consists of a layer of limestone blocks that have been altered in place. The matrix of Bed N is a clayey sand with medium-sized blocks of limestone. The greenish clays of Bed N were labeled by the Henri-Martins as Bed 3. Bed M is the deepest layer to be excavated by Jelinek and Debénath; the brownish yellow clay contains high numbers of large faunal elements with few chipped stone artifacts. Bed L is a light gray-brown clay deposit with a higher density of both bone and stone artifacts than Bed M.

The middle section as defined in the recent excavations comprises deposits from the top of Bed K to the base of Bed 8. These layers roughly correspond to Beds 1 and 2 as defined by the Henri-Martins. The strata are not horizontal, they are occasionally consolidated and somewhat deformed. Unlike the basal sediments which are essentially fluvial in nature, the matrix of the middle beds is derived from the slope above or from *in situ* weathering of limestone clasts. Excavations in the middle layers have been limited. In 1987, several half meter-squares were opened against the northeastern face of Trench C to provide a clean, vertical profile (Debénath and Jelinek 1987).

Beds F - K are similar to Germaine Henri-Martin's 2b and 2c. Bed J is defined as a thin lens of light brown calcareous sand while K is distinguished from J by the inclusion of medium *éboulis* (10 cm). Beds G and H are cemented calcareous sands with small (3-5 cm) rounded limestone fragments. Bed H and the three subdivisions of Bed G are distinguished by minor variations in color and *éboulis* size. Although the deposits are moderately inclined toward the river valley, several articulated reindeer bones have been recovered from these rich archaeological layers. These deposits accord with Dr. Henri-Martin's "organic pocket" containing an "evolved" Mousterian industry.

Bed F is colluvium that was probably derived from the upper terraces and the plateau at the top of the cliff. The reddish-brown clay at the top of this stratum contains few signs of cultural occupation and seems to post-date the formation of an anomaly near the cliff face. These slumped deposits can be recognized in Dr. Henri-Martin's section (Fig. 4) and in his daughter's drawing of the same profile (Fig. 5). The feature appears to have been formed when the upper part of Bed G was

drawn down in front of the cliff face. This feature might have been formed during the period of earthquake-induced landslides envisioned by Alimen (1951). Jelinek (1990a) has suggested a cryogenic explanation for this geological anomaly, but no definitive examination of the feature has been conducted. The anomaly was subsequently filled and capped by a deep layer of sterile colluvium near the cliff face which is included in the description of Bed F. Although Bed F is thin and patchy near the limits of the slope, this colluvium is massive at the rear of the site and forms the base of the upper "midden" strata (Jelinek 1988b).

At the base of the slope Bed E contains a layer of large limestone blocks with little sediment or archaeological material. This rocky stratum appears to truncate earlier deposits. Bed D is comprised of clayey-sandy silt with various sizes of limestone fragments. Bed C has medium to large *éboulis* within the context of unstructured gray sediments. Cultural material and limestone fragments in this stratum are aligned with the slope, suggesting some vertical movement. Bed C appears to be contiguous with Bed 8 in the upper sequence of beds. The larger quantity of archaeological material in Bed C gives it a darker, more organic hue than Bed D.

Beds A and B are sterile strata that cover the lower slope of the site but pinch out near the base of the upper beds. The yellow-brown colluvium of Bed A contains a number of limestone blocks and fragments that follow the pitch of the slope. Bed B is defined as a layer of medium-sized (10 cm) limestone fragments at the base of Bed A. Beds A and B are equivalent to Germaine Henri-Martin's Bed 1a and may post-date the deposits of the upper "midden" beds (Beds 2 through 8).

These upper strata include deposits over a meter in depth that contain a large quantity of cultural material (Fig. 7). The beds are horizontal and extend out from the cliff face as much as five meters. Continuity with the sloping deposits of Bed C from this platform and the density of the archaeological material in the upper beds may indicate that the horizontal surface of colluvium underlying Bed 8 was man-made (G. Henri-Martin 1976). At this height, the limestone face forms a slight overhang. The overhang seems to be more pronounced to the northeast toward the center of the remaining nine meters of deposits. Test excavations suggest that an overhang of as much as two meters may exist at the center of the deposits. The very high density of cultural material in these upper levels may reflect more intense use of the site during this time than during the deposition of the middle and lower beds. At times the proportion of animal bone and flint in these strata is equal to, or greater than, the proportion of actual sediment, giving the impression of a "midden" or domestic refuse deposit. These layers correspond to Germaine Henri-Martin's "last Mousterian habitat".

Beds 7 and 8 form the base of these upper horizontal deposits. Bed 8 is the darkest and most heavily organic layer in this section at La Quina. Enormous quantities of predominantly reindeer bone are mixed with fine sediments, very small rounded limestone fragments and numbers of flint artifacts.

Bed 7 contrasts with the other upper strata in its white-yellow color. The sediment is grainy and calcareous with small to medium rounded *éboulis* clasts and appears to represent a period of *in situ* disintegration of frost-fractured limestone.

Bed 6 is a dense horizonal accumulation over 50 cm deep that has been subdivided into four layers. The entire group of deposits is a very dark gray due to quantities of burned, broken bone. Contrary to the Henri-Martins' interpretations, no intact hearth areas have been recognized and the proportion of lithics is relatively high. Bed 6D, the basal subdivision within Bed 6, includes of a number of medium-sized limestone fragments mixed with fine sediments. The deposits of 6C are distinguished by fewer and smaller *éboulis* fragments and a higher proportion of burned material than 6D. Bed 6B is a very thin lens of medium to small rounded limestone pebbles that is spatially restricted to a small area near the cliff. Bed 6A has small, rounded *éboulis* fragments (average 2.5 cm) with fine dark interstitial sediment. In 1988 an unusual feature was encountered in the upper deposits (Fig. 10). The edge of a pit with large limestone slabs in its interior was found. The 65 by 85 cm pit was dug from Bed 6A down to the top of Bed 8, a depth of approximately 60 cm. The pit was filled with 30 large limestone blocks (up to 10 kg each) and loosely packed midden material; the fill was labeled Bed 6A1 during excavation.

Layers 1 - 5 are present in a small area adjacent to the cliff at the top of the site. Unlike the relatively large horizontal expanse of Beds 7 and 8, layer 5 extends a maximum of 2.5 meters from the cliff face. Beds 4 - 2 occupy an even smaller space up to and under the cliff overhang.

Bed 5 is a thin layer of tabular limestone fragments that have been slightly rounded on their edges. Bed 4 is composed primarily of small fragments of frost-cracked limestone (*éboulis*) with little intersticial sediment. The majority of the fragments are smaller than 3 cm, although some pieces have a diameter up to 5 cm. The stratum is rich in large bone fragments, but lithic artifacts are rare. Bed 4 has been divided into two layers: 4A and 4B. A horizontal layer of large limestone blocks designated as Bed 3 overlies these cultural remains. Some of the blocks have been frost cracked in place. Bed 3 contains very little sediment and very few faunal elements between its limestone fragments. Bed 2 is a yellow clayey sand with large angular fragments of collapsed limestone in its upper half (2A). The limestone fragments in the lower half (2B) are much smaller and more rounded. Cultural remains, especially faunal remains, are minimal in layer 2, but are more apparent in 2B. Large, often articulated bone fragments of equids and bovids are found in Bed 2B as in Bed 4B. Many of the bones have been shattered and compressed by the subsequent rockfall of 2A. Bed 1 is a thin layer of dark humic soil with a low density of cultural material that covers the entire surface of the slope.

CULTURAL AND ENVIRONMENTAL RECONSTRUCTION
Sedimentology
The absence of absolute dating techniques for the majority of the Middle Paleolithic period has prompted the need for a means of relative chronological control. Study of sediments has been integral in the French archaeological analyses, particularly in the prehistory of Southwest France. The limestone plateaus of this region are subject to extensive weathering. The formation of rockshelters by cryoclastic erosion and the subsequent alteration of the deposits have been examined in detail by Henri Laville (1973; Laville *et al.* 1980). Climatic reconstructions from geological analysis have then been correlated with other environmental indicators and linked to major glacial cycles of the Middle Paleolithic.

These methods of paleoclimatic analysis have been applied extensively to limestone formations and rock shelters in Southwest France. Coarser blocks of limestone with little sediment indicate deposition under conditions of severe cold, while smaller fragments with more intersticial matrix indicate less rigorous conditions. Sedimentological studies are best used as guidelines to be supported by other climatic indicators such as faunal identification or pollen analysis. Sedimentology is useful for building relative chronologies within sites, but regional correlations of deposits are extremely difficult. Each series of deposits is subject to a range of primary and secondary factors including temperature, humidity, variation in cycles of freezing and thawing, and vegetation growth. Local environmental factors such as site and valley orientation also affect the alteration of limestone blocks and fragments. Effects of individual erosional factors can rarely be distinguished, but sedimentology can provide an idea of relative conditions over a period of time. The texture and composition of the deposits at La Quina reflect the actions of frozen and running water in a number of ways that will be explored later in this chapter.

Faunal Identification
The site of La Quina is known for its incredible density of faunal remains. Reconstructions of climate and site activity are often based upon these remains. As recognized by the Henri-Martins, the fauna at La Quina is comprised primarily of reindeer, horse and bovid. While the relative proportions of these three genera fluctuates between strata, the numbers of other species remains very low. The reindeer have been identified as *Rangifer tarandus* and the equids as *Equus caballus*, but the bovids are less precisely classified. The specimens may be *Bos primigenius* or *Bison priscus*, but *Bison* seems to predominate (Armand n.d.). *Cervus elaphus*, red deer, is also present in significant quantities in some beds.

Reindeer in Dr. Henri-Martin's Bed 4 were the earliest faunal remains associated with cultural material recognized at La Quina. Excavations up to 1991 had not adequately sampled the basal units (Beds Q-N) for comparative information. Dr. Henri-Martin (1923b) noted a high number of antlers in this basal stratum and hypothesized about conditions of severe cold for this context. Alimen's (1951) analysis of these sediments also suggested waning intense cold for this period.

Quantities of animal bones havebeen recovered from Bed M up to Bed 2A by each excavation team. Beds L and M are paricularly rich in large bones of reindeer, horse, and bovid. The bone fragments are not articulated, but do represent all parts of the skeleton. Beds 2B and 4B at the top of the

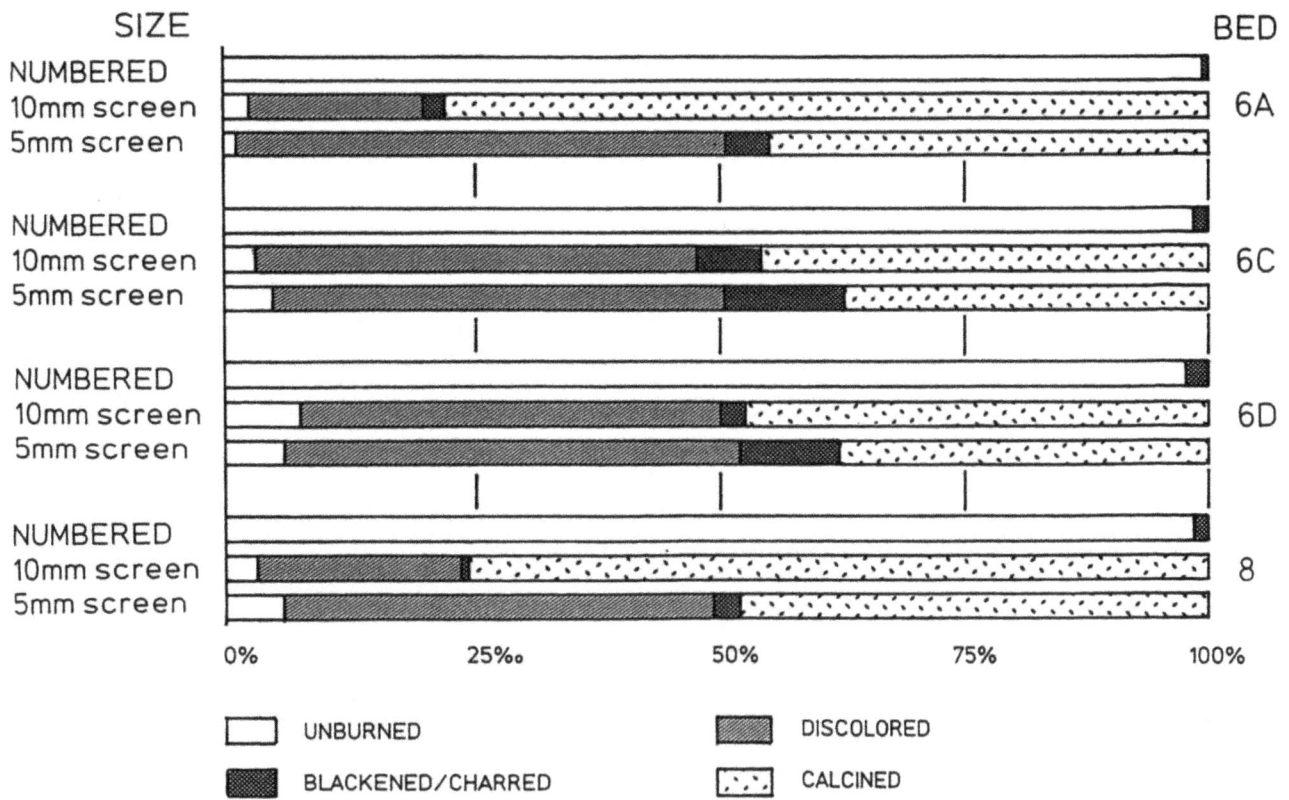

Figure 10. Stages of burning of bone fragments graded by size (Chase in Jelinek 1990:21)

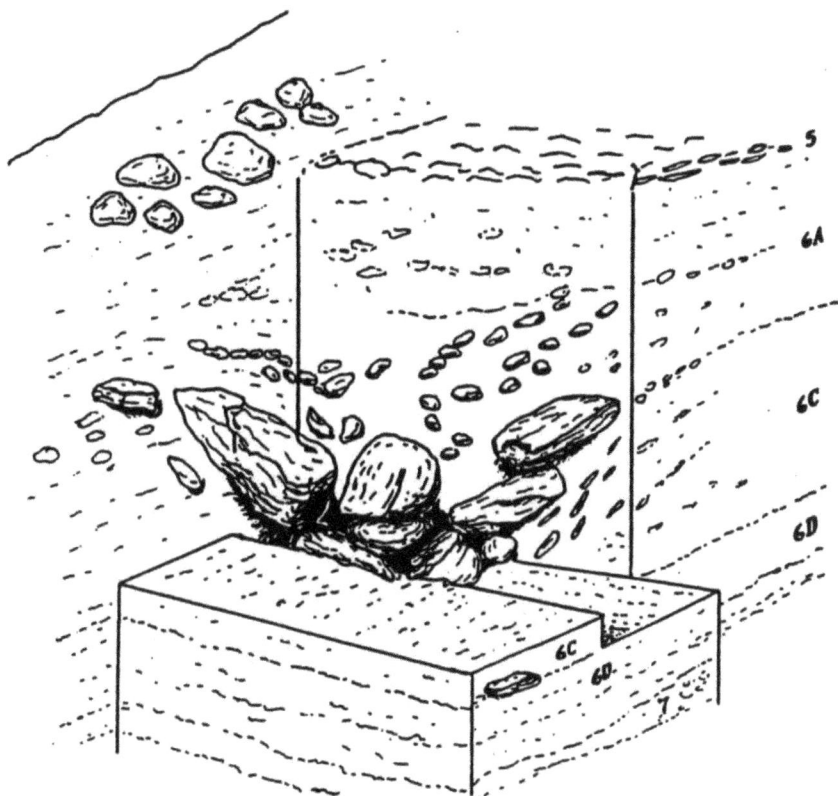

Figure 11. Isometric diagram of structure ST1 (Jelinek 1990)

sequence also contain a faunal assemblage of large bone fragments that are occasionally articulated. The presence of axial skeletal parts here suggests minimal transport of the animal carcasses. These two pairs of beds contain the highest frequencies of bone to stone at the site. Lithic artifacts comprise less than 25 per cent of the artifacts found in these deposits. (Jelinek 1990a).

Between these extreme stratigraphic positions, animal bone occurs in smaller pieces and lower proportions. Although the sample from the middle levels is limited, several articulated reindeer bones have been recovered along with numerous unburned bone fragments. The faunal assemblage from the midden levels in the upper sectyion is extremely dense. Quantities of burned and unburned bone fragments are mixed together. Chase (n.d.)(Fig. 11) has analyzed the bone from the sample columns in these upper beds and suggests two distinct modes of origin. Larger pieces of bone were not exposed to fire, while smaller bone fragments are often burned. Chase argues that the large unburned bones represent *in situ* butchering, while the small, burned bone fragments might be derived from the upper terraces. The faunal assemblages from Beds 6 and 7 contain a mixture of bovid, equid and reindeer bones, but the Bed 8 assemblage is dominated by reindeer.

All three of the major faunal taxa represented at La Quina are herd animals that at present live in relatively open country. Although reindeer can survive more rigorous conditions than equids or bovids, all of these animals can adapt to relatively cold conditions. Delpech *et al.* (1983) have classified reindeer as inhabitants of open arctic ranges, while horse and bison are most often associated with an open non-arctic ecosystem. Through the analysis of faunal assemblages from other French Middle Paleolithic sites, they have found that animals associated with one climatological regime tend to dominate a given stratum at a site except during periods of transition. Jelinek (1987) has conducted preliminary examinations that suggest that bovids are most common at the base of the section, reindeer predominate in the middle and lower portion of the upper levels, and horse bones are most frequently encountered in the final deposits (Beds 6-2). Using these faunal variations as paleoclimatic indicators, a generally cold regime with an intermediate phase of increasingly intense cold can be postulated for the occupational episodes at La Quina.

Pollen Studies
Pollen samples were taken by Renault-Miskovski in 1987, 1989 and 1991. The first samples taken from the basal strata were not suitable for analysis. Another series of pollen samples for the lower beds and an initial series for the middle beds were procured during the 1991 field season. The pollen from the upper deposits collected in 1987 and 1989 included some arboreal elements in Bed 8 and indicated an increase in forest species, especially hazelnut and fern, throughout the deposition of the upper strata (Renault-Miskovski 1990).

Climatic Reconstruction and Site Use
Preliminary studies in geology, zoology, palynology and archaeology can be correlated to create a picture of events at La Quina during the Late Pleistocene. Since there are no absolute dates for the early periods of cultural activity at La Quina, relative chronological indicators must be used. A sequence of cutting and filling for the nearby Isle River (Fig. 1) has been developed by Texier *et al.* (1983). The final erosional episode for this valley has been correlated to the Riss-Würm interglacial. This temperate climatic phase, also known as Stage 5e in the oxygen isotope record, has been dated to approximately 125,000 BP (Laville *et al.* 1983, Shackleton and Opdyke 1973). In Texier *et al*'s analysis, water flowing from melting glaciers incised the landscape on its way to the ocean. The rapidly flowing stream may have scoured the Isle River valley and widened its floodplain at this time. Excavation of the basal strata at La Quina shows that similar scouring may have occurred in the Voultron Valley.

Since similar episodes of cutting and filling have not characterized the present interglacial regime in this region, alternative explanations must also be considered. Lowered ocean levels during glacial maxima could have been responsible for long term headword erosion of these river valleys. This downcutting from the west could have incised the Voultron River Valley before or after the last interglacial rather than during a temperate phase.

Once the Voultron Valley had been incised, limestone fragments began to weather from the cliff face, creating a wedge of talus blocks. At the same time, the stream deposited several layers of sand and clay at the edge of the valley. Some smaller fragments of *éboulis* became incorporated into these deposits. The fluvial sediments indicate that the river was at a high level, although the small size of the sediment grains suggest slow water movement, perhaps from repeated gentle flooding. In the valley of the Isle 50 kilometers from the Voultron, Texier *et al.* (1983) found similar evidence of ponding represented by a deposit of peat that rests upon the Riss-Würm terrace. Although limestone weathering was continuous during the deposition of the basal units at La Quina, the climate was probably not terribly severe. Shell samples were taken from these sands by Germaine Henri-Martin (1976), but were not climatically diagnostic. As noted, pollen samples were taken by Renault-Miskovski from these beds in 1987 and 1991, but both were unproductive.

During excavation of the basal units, faunal elements have been recovered as low as Bed N. The stratum contains bones of equids, bovids and reindeer with scattered lithic artifacts. Bed M is a similar clay deposit with large broken bones and a limited number of stone tools, all of which are stained reddish-brown by manganese and iron oxides. The sparse lithic assemblage is primarily comprised of large scrapers, large flakes, and a number of quartz cobbles. The assemblage would be defined as a Quina Mousterian industry. The undulating contact between these clayey beds suggests a boggy environment at the margin of the floodplain. Jelinek (1990a) has proposed that La Quina served as primary butchering site during this period. Animals could have been frightened over the cliff or simply mired in marshy areas and butchered *in situ*. He suggests that the relatively large tool size can be accounted for by loss in the boggy sediments. Dr. Henri-Martin recognized extensive use of bone for tools in these strata

(1907). Numerous bone fragments were fashioned and abraded as tools in lithic reduction (Boëda and Vincent 1990, Armand personal communication 1991). Unutilized bones in these basal layers are generally recovered in large, disarticulated pieces. As the bones do not show evidence of water abrasion or sorting they were probably rapidly covered by slow-moving stream deposits.

Above the basal strata, the nature of deposition changes. The sediments are not fluvial in nature but colluvial. The middle beds contain higher proportions of broken and abraded limestone and lower percentages of clays and silts. These layers continued to accumulate in front of, and on top of, the talus cone slope. Although most of the non-cultural material is believed to have come down from the cliff terraces, the derivation of the cultural material is less clear. Lenticular concentrations of cultural material are present in these layers of colluvium and *éboulis*. The bone and stone artifacts are aligned with the slope, but the recovery of articulated reindeer bones in Bed G suggests that little displacement occurred between butchering and deposition. Higher percentages of reindeer bone in these middle strata are an indicator of increasingly cold conditions, but the size and texture of the limestone fragments do not suggest conditions of extreme dry cold. The lithic assemblage in these middle strata resembles that of the lower units and would again be called a Quina Mousterian industry, but the artifacts here are smaller and more intensively retouched than below. Jelinek (1988b) suggests that the differences in lithic size between the lower and middle units can be explained by a change in site environment rather than a change in site use. La Quina may still have been primarily a butchering site, but these tools were discarded when fully spent rather than lost during use.

Bed F represents the redeposition of colluvium from above. The reddish color of the patchy sediments at the top of Bed F indicates development of vegetation on the upper terraces and cliff top during a warmer period. Given the faunal indications of increasing cold throughout this period, this soil development may have occurred at an earlier point in time and terminated with the onset of severe climatic conditions. Cementing in Beds G and H would support the presence of more humic acids in runoff coming from soil formation on the upper terraces. The collapse of Bed G sediments near the cliff face prior to the deposition of Bed F has yet to be fully explained. This anomaly may have been the result of frost action. The massive colluvium of Bed F and a layer of large angular limestone blocks in Bed E indicate continued conditions of intense dry cold. Jelinek (1988b) suggests that this period of severe cold may correlate with the Würm II cold peak also known from oxygen isotope cores as Stage 4, dated to approximately 70,000 BP.

The overlying slope deposits are mixtures of colluvium, *éboulis,* and cultural material. The size and texture of the limestone fragments indicate an ameliorating climate with shorter cycles of freeze-thaw. As noted previously, the base of Bed 8 rests upon a horizontal platform at the top of the massive colluvium that overlies Bed F. If the leveling of this platform was not a natural occurrence, some of the deposits of Bed C may represent redeposition of sediment that had been pushed down the slope from the apex of the profile. The thin strata of Beds A and B may have accumulated on the slope during or after the deposition of the upper beds.

As stated above, the faunal assemblage in Bed 8 is dominated by reindeer bones. The dense mass of bones and bone fragments includes all parts of the reindeer carcass. Although the limited sediment in this layer is not climatically diagnostic, the domination of reindeer bones and frost damage to the bones (Guadelli personal communication 1991) indicate continued severe cold. A hiatus in cultural deposition concurrent with a layer of limestone collapse is evidence for an interval of even more intense cold after the deposition of Bed 8. This *éboulis* weathered in place to form Bed 7. The granularity of the white limestone pieces and the intersticial sediment within Bed 7 indicate the onset of a slightly moderated climate after this period of intense cold.

The sediments and artifacts in Bed 6 also indicate less severe climatic conditions. First, limited amounts of *éboulis* occur in small, rounded fragments. Increased arboreal elements in these pollen samples also suggest the presence of climatic moderation. Finally, the faunal assemblage for Bed 6 suggests a transition to less severe conditions. The bones of horse and bison predominate, with fewer reindeer. Microfauna has been recovered from Bed 6 sediments. These bones may represent detritus from raptors in overhead branches. The microvertebrate bones have not yet been analyzed for precise climatological indications.

The high cultural content in the upper beds suggests relatively rapid accumulation. The midden-like layers appear to represent a different form of site use at La Quina - habitation rather than sporadic butchering activity. The lithic assemblages are more varied and less reduced. All of the upper beds have a number of denticulate and notched tools; each would be classified as a Denticulate Mousterian industry with the exception of Bed 6D. The presence of bifacially flaked hand axes in this context classifies it as a MTA industry. Burned bones have been fragmented into extremely small pieces and mixed with unburned ones. The absence of well-defined hearths and the horizontal nature of the mixed cultural material in Beds 8 and 6 suggests redeposition of domestic debris. Burned bone and lithic fragments have been moved enough to break and separate, but not enough to cause abrasion or rounding. The direction of movement, horizontal or vertical, has not yet been ascertained.

The rapid accumulation of the midden deposits is confirmed by a series of absolute dates. These "last Mousterian habitat" layers at La Quina were dated by Germaine Henri-Martin (1964) to 35,250 ± 530 BP (GrN 2526). Jelinek (1990a) has had a series of TAMS (Tandem Math Accelerator) dates run on bulk collagen from three unburned bone samples from the same upper level contexts. The bone from Bed 8 has been dated to 34,200 ± 700 BP (AA-3637), Bed 6C to 34,450 ± 725 BP (AA-3638) and Bed 4B to 34,130 ± 700 BP (AA-3639). These three accelerator dates do not differ significantly from one another nor do they differ from the date on bone obtained by

Germaine Henri-Martin.

The structure, Bed 6A1, appears to have been dug from Bed 6A down to the top of Bed 8. As the artifact inventory for this feature is a mixture of bone, stone and sediment not unlike the surrounding matrix, it has not yet helped reveal the function of the pit. Jelinek (1990a) has proposed that the pit was used periodically for meat storage. The meat could have been cached in the winter and covered with rocks for protection from scavengers. In the spring the meat could have been removed and the rocks replaced to maintain the form of the pit for future use. Similar features have been encountered in Middle Paleolithic excavations by Peyrony at Le Moustier (1930) and by Bordes at Combe Grenal (1972). Based upon the skeletal remains recovered by Peyrony at Le Moustier, Bordes suggested that the structures might have been used for infant burial although he did not recover any human bone or unusual artifacts in pit excavation at Combe Grenal. Detailed examination of the lithic assemblage from the pit fill in this analysis may shed more light on its function.

Bed 6 is capped by a layer of limestone slabs labeled Bed 5. The beds above the limestone are more similar to the basal units than to the middle or other upper ones. They reflect periods of limestone collapse and minimal weathering, alternating with occasional cultural use up to the top of the profile. The small area up to and under the cliff face would not have been suitable for occupation, but the cultural material is packed under the cliff overhang in a manner that suggests that it was not derived from above. Remains of butchering activity again predominate. Large and sometimes articulated pieces of equid, bovid and reindeer bone are accompanied by limited numbers of flint tools, especially denticulate and notched tools, and quartz pebbles.

The entire sequence is capped by a thin deposit of organic debris (Bed 1). This superficial layer of dark colluvium, humus and limestone fragments covers the entire slope. The Station Amont at La Quina does not contain any evidence of cultural activity after the filling of the small shelter. If any later activity occurred, it has been subject to erosion.

Prehistoric Site Use
The intensive and extensive cultural remains at La Quina have often been linked to its unusual geographical situation (Henri-Martin 1923a, 1923b, 1936; Jelinek *et al.* 1989). The site lies at the foot of a high, steep cliff that rises more than 20 meters above the valley floor (Fig. 2). From the top, the scarp is not visible; the wide, rolling hills seem to continue unbroken. This unusual feature has been posited to have served as a natural hunting aid. Dr. Henri-Martin felt that the cliffs might have been used as a natural trap by Mousterian hunters because they lacked the tools to kill large fauna or to dig pits (1936). A similar function is proposed by Jelinek, Debénath, and Dibble (1989). They argue that since the largest concentration of animal bone is below the highest cliff scarp of the region and since the majority of animal bone found at La Quina is that of gregarious animals (reindeer, horse and bison), it is likely that the animals were frightened over the cliff and butchered below. Unlike faunal assemblages at game drive sites (e.g. Scottsbluff:

Barbour and Schultz 1932), the faunal remains at La Quina were relatively completely disarticulated and apparently fully utilized. The faunal remains at the Station Amont do not represent massive group slaughter but rather a series of repeated kills of a few animals. Because there is no evidence for large game drives, it is difficult to prove whether a few animals were driven from above and consumed below or whether they were trapped in other ways.

The location of the site of La Quina may be explained by the use of the plateau above the locus as a natural game trap, but an alternative interpretation can be made by focusing on the base of the scarp. The site is located at the only point in the valley where abrupt cliffs are opposed (Fig. 2). At every other point along the valley one side or the other is opened by sloping hills or the entrance of a tributary. The ability to restrict the valley at both ends with cairns, fires, other devices, or human activity would have been a great advantage in hunting. This hypothesis is most difficult to prove for the upper deposits at La Quina. At the very top of the section, the recovery of large articulated bones would suggest that carcasses had been dragged 10 meters uphill if they had not fallen from above. The dense concentration of bone at La Quina implies that the site was an especially favorable place to hunt. Hypotheses about the site's function must consider the morphology of the base of the cliff as well as its position below a steep scarp. Chase's (personal communication 1991) analysis of burned bone fragments suggests that at least two modes of deposition are responsible for the accumulation of cultural material at this site, and several means of hunting could have been used at this locality as well.

Conclusion
An interpretation of cultural activity at La Quina has been developed by each principal investigator at the site. Studies of the geological and archaeological record have helped to expose variation in the depositional environment and in site use. Sedimentology, palynology, and faunal identification are used to reflect climatic conditions. The oldest layers at La Quina appear to have been deposited in a cold, moist environment. Decreased levels of precipitation and extremely cold temperatures characterize the period of deposition for the middle and early upper beds. Finally, a cool and more humid climate seems to have prevailed during the deposition of the final, upper strata.

Variation in bone and stone artifacts have been used to indicate changes in cultural activities at La Quina. In the basal beds activity seems to have centered upon the use of even edged tools in the butchering of large game. Assemblages from the upper beds at La Quina indicate that a broader range of activities took place. Animal bones still form a significant part of the cultural remains, but the fragments are much smaller and more frequently burned. The retouched tools in the upper beds are more varied than below. These lines of evidence may indicate the presence of longer periods of occupation at La Quina during the deposition of the upper beds, perhaps phases of semi-permanent habitation.

Each of the investigators at La Quina has developed similar hypotheses about site use and environment. More detailed analysis of the limestone, bone, and unretouched stone objects will help to clarify these theories. This study attempts to reveal changes in patterns of tool and core manufacture and reduction through the analysis of the entire lithic assemblage including, but not limited to, the retouched tool component. Other studies of the La Quina materials may elucidate the kinds of activities conducted at the site as well as the original location for such activities.

Chapter IV

PROJECT RESEARCH DESIGN

Introduction

Shaped stone and worked bone are the only artifacts recovered from the first two million years of the cultural record. While other types of artifacts can disappear from the archaeological record, lithics remain relatively unchanged. The durability, sharp edges, and availability of stone made it a useful material prehistorically and the only ubiquitous modern guide to prehistoric behavior. As suggested by Toth (1987b), lithic technology is the most completely preserved system in prehistory. Archaeologists attempt to understand prehistoric technology, subsistence, and lifeways from these lithic remains. For the most part analysis is conducted on retouched chipped stone artifacts, or tools. Although stone tools were undoubtedly economically important to prehistoric peoples, these broken and discarded objects found in sites do not accurately reflect a functioning tool kit or the full sequence of lithic manufacture and reduction (Frison 1968, Jelinek 1976). The present study was designed to incorporate all classes of recovered stone including tools as well as products of lithic manufacture and maintenance to obtain a fuller understanding of prehistoric lifeways. The sample was taken from material recovered in the 1985-1990 excavations at La Quina.

Middle Paleolithic Typology

Because stone artifacts and faunal remains are essentially the only surviving record of behavior in the Middle Paleolithic, the significance of lithic variability has been central to interpretation of the cultural record. As discussed in Chapter II, most debate has focused on the relative importance of style and function and their relationship to diachronic and synchronic variability in tool form (Bordes and de Sonneville-Bordes 1970; Binford and Binford 1966).

> Difficulties in convincingly relating lithic variability to past behavior may be due, in considerable part, to an underlying paradigm that structures not only the way in which both sides of the debate view lithics, but pervades most interpretations of stone artifacts (Barton 1991:144)

Barton's (1988, 1989) industrial paradigm points out the differences between modern tools and stone ones. Modern industrial tools are fabricated from metal allowing for more specificity in function and style. Secondly, metal tools do not change with use. Conversely, the production of stone tools is not necessarily as goal-oriented as modern tool production and the end product in stone is not as morphologically stable as that produced in metal. Technological limitations of chipped stone require the manufacture of more generalized forms. The mechanics of flint knapping restrict the range of tool blank shapes, and functional areas of lithic tools are limited to their edges. Unlike industrial tools, chipped stone artifacts may be produced to meet a number of unspecified needs (Kelly 1988). Finally, because chipped stone must be refurbished to remain useful, the analysis of tools from archaeological sites reflects the end of an object's use life, not its function over time (Frison 1968).

Although cores, flakes, and shatter have been included in lithic analyses, most classifications and interpretations are still based on tools. Using the modern industrial paradigm, tools are expected to segregate into classes and to reflect changes in style and function. Groups of similar artifacts are delineated by sets of attributes (i.e. edge morphology, blank type, flaking technique). These groups, or classes, are described from an idealized type but include a range of variation. The variability of each attribute is often more continuous than discrete. For example, the utilitarian parts of a tool, its edges, are theoretically either even or serrated. In reality, the edge may reflect any condition between these two extremes or a combination of forms.

Despite problems with typological classification, the interpretation of Middle Paleolithic cultural patterns has relied almost entirely on tool analysis. The typology developed by Francois Bordes (1950a, 1953, 1961) has served as a baseline for communication and analysis in Middle Paleolithic lithic studies since its inception. His classification system for tools and some classes of debitage is still widely used to characterize Middle Paleolithic assemblages, but archaeologists have begun to include other types of analysis in their studies. Studies of debitage have added greatly to the understanding of cultural activity in prehistory. Analysis of tools within this broader context has resulted in less emphasis on strict typological classification. The inclusion of debitage in lithic analyses has a number of advantages over studies of tools alone. As noted by Frison (1968), flakes are not as likely to be culturally or naturally transported as tools. Debitage is also usually relatively abundant in archaeological sites. Finally,

> debitage retains evidence of prior manufacturing steps, thus its variability must in some ways be related directly to the formal variability of intended products of manufacture (Magne 1989:15).

Debitage analysis can show what kinds of tools were used at a site and which parts of the reduction sequence were practiced. Reduction processes can then be examined in relation to raw material procurement, site function, and subsistence patterns.

Limitations of Interpretation

Analyses of lithic reduction sequences can be used to examine technological variability, but the interpretation of such variability is limited by three major variables: the material properties of stone, archaeological context, and reliance upon ethnographic analogy (Close 1989). First, as previously noted, the material properties of stone and the technology available to form lithic objects are extremely restrictive. Yet a great deal of behavioral interpretation is still based on the relatively small range of potential variation in lithic form and technique.

Second, the archaeological context of lithic material may limit its interpretation. Poor contextual resolution and an absence of absolute dates compound problems in the interpretation of Middle Paleolithic assemblages. The dense midden-like strata at La Quina impose severe limitations to cultural interpretation.

The material represents a mixture of a number of occupations over time whose deposition cannot be separated or dated. Although some of the lower and middle strata at La Quina are fine, distinct layers, the upper "midden" beds contain quantities of burned and unburned bone mixed with quantities of lithic remains in strata up to 30 cm thick. The basal layers have better defined geological strata and may represent less intense site use than the upper deposits, but these artifacts were still subject to post-depositional movement and mixing.

The third limitation to lithic interpretation is the reliance on ethnographic analogy for behavioral correlates. Technology, subsistence, mobility, and territoriality are terms familiar to the archaeologist through studies of modern hunter-gatherer groups. Ethnographic data and models can be useful for some correlations, but scholars of the Middle Paleolithic cannot assume that Neanderthals behaved in the same ways as fully modern humans (Clark 1968, Freeman 1968). Although most archaeologists would agree that Neanderthals are not too far distant genetically from anatomically modern humans, the size and robustness of Neanderthals would certainly have affected their subsistence needs and acquisition methods (Stringer and Gamble 1993). The magnitude and significance of these biological differences has not yet been quantified. The behavior and abstract mental capacities of Neanderthals is another unknown limiting the interpretation of Middle Paleolithic remains (Chase and Dibble 1987; Clark and Lindley 1989a, 1998b). Reconstructing prehistoric behavior through ethnographic analogy is not futile, but archaeologists must be aware of the limitations of such inferences. Middle Paleolithic hominids were physically different, perhaps mentally different, and certainly inhabited an environment unlike that of modern hunter-gather groups.

Lithic Analysis at La Quina

Interpretation of inter- and intra-site lithic patterning in the Middle Paleolithic has been particularly focused in two areas: (1) distinguishing between function and ethnicity as the forces governing variability, and (2) recognizing reduction strategies and linking these to systems of economy and settlement (Henry and Odell 1989). While the former debate has proven to be less than fruitful, the latter objective is helping archaeologists to better understand prehistoric subsistence and lithic variability. For the purposes of this study, the full assemblage of excavated lithics from La Quina was analyzed in an attempt to discern such variation. The small flakes, chunks and shatter were included in analysis in order to flesh out the picture of prehistoric subsistence. Variations in attributes such as flake size, shape, cortex, and platform morphology are used to expose differences in technique and intensity of lithic reduction and manufacture. This variation is linked to patterns of mobility and raw material acquisition.

In order to detect technological patterning between strata at La Quina, samples were taken from the lower, middle and upper sets of beds. Although excavation as of 1990 had not been extensive enough to recover an adequate sample from every stratum, several beds from each group of deposits were included in the sample. All of the material excavated through the 1990 season from the basal units (Beds L - M) was included. These lithics were recovered from a thin lens in six

meter-square units and include 157 individually recorded artifacts from Bed M and 447 from Bed L (Fig. 6). The assemblage for the middle layers was recovered from narrow excavations along the southwestern face of Germaine Henri-Martin's surviving section. Lithics from Beds C - G came from the excavation of three half meter-square units and include 748 individually recorded artifacts from Beds G, 166 from Bed E, 161 from Bed D, and 87 from Bed C. The lithic assemblage from three square meters of the upper deposits (Beds 4B - 8) was also analyzed. As excavations have been most extensive at the top of the profile, only a part of the recovered material was examined; six half meter-squares were included in this sample. These assemblages were chosen to sample three areas along the upper profile: against the cliff wall, in the middle of the midden deposits, and at the front edge of the deposits to examine variation in assemblages over time and space has been analyzed. The sample of individually recorded artifacts for Bed 8 is 1047, 248 for Bed 7, 986 for Bed 6D, 671 for Bed 6C, 793 for Bed 6A and 423 for Bed 4B. All of the recovered material from the pit feature in Bed 6A1 was examined; data on 458 individually recorded artifacts from Bed 6A1 was recorded.

The research design included three methods of lithic collection and analysis. These three types of analysis were included to ensure coverage and control of the lithic sample. First, all of the large (over 3 cm), numbered artifacts were recorded individually. Identifiable pieces of tools or cores and flakes of reduction or modification were culled from the 50 cm excavation and screen bags; these artifacts were recorded in the same manner as artifacts individually numbered on site and were included in the same data set. Each of the individually recorded artifacts were classified using a series of sixteen variables (Appendices I and II). These artifacts make up the samples described in the previous paragraph. The second level of analysis involved the remaining flakes in each level bag from 50 cm excavation units and screened sediments. These flakes were sorted by material, completeness and exterior cortex. The bag for each level and unit was counted and weighed as a whole. The final stage of data collection focused on three control columns. All of the material from a series of 10 x 10 x 5 cm sediment samples from the upper deposits was subjected to complete collection in nested screens (10 mm, 5 mm, 2 mm, 0.5 mm). The large lithic artifacts were analyzed in the same way as the numbered artifacts. The smaller flakes and fragments were sorted, counted and weighed as a group. The number of lithics in each graded screen was also noted. The lithics, soil, limestone and bone portions of the samples were weighed for controlled comparison of natural and anthropogenic content. In 1991, two samples each of the same size (10 x 10 x 5 cm) were taken from Beds G and M; these four samples have been included with the column samples.

Data on the individual artifacts was recorded using a program written by Harold Dibble and Shannon McPherron. The variables in the data entry program were revised by the author for the purposes of this lithic analysis. The sixteen variables (Appendix I) are based in part upon concepts of lithic analysis utilized by Bordes (1961), Jelinek (1977a), Fish (1979) and Frison (1968). Some variables are measures of a single attribute, but most represent a typological selection involving a number of attributes.

A total of 6500 artifacts were classified using the sixteen variables and 6392 are included in this study. A number of artifacts from beds with limited lithic material were not able to be utilized. Over 125 bags of flakes from excavation and screening were sorted, counted and weighed and a total of nineteen 10 x 10 x 5 cm samples from six beds were sorted and examined. The data were transferred to DBase for sorting and counting. These counts were tallied and frequencies calculated with the assistance of Lotus 1-2-3. Statistical computations were conducted in a basic analysis program written by Arthur Jelinek.

Attributes

Each object was classified as a flake, tool, core or chunk. Flakes are defined as artifacts having a single interior face with no intentional retouch. Tools are retouched artifacts, usually made on flakes. Cores are artifacts with one or more negative flake scars and usually lacking an interior face, while chunks are defined by an absence of clear positive or negative flake scars. Given the high density of anthropogenic material and near absence of natural stone in the sediments, all siliceous and quartz objects were considered to be cultural in nature.

The next observation was made on material. Each object was judged to have been manufactured out of flint, quartz (or quartzite), jasper, or another material. Although different types of flint were used at La Quina, analysis of these raw material sources could not be integrated with this technological analysis. Primary sourcing is being carried out by Christine Kervaso of the Center for Prehistory in Perigeux in a manner similar to studies by Geneste (1985). These two data sets will eventually be integrated for publication in final reports on La Quina.

In order to have data on proportions of raw material for the entire La Quina assemblage, all flakes were divided by material. The bags of flakes from screening and excavation by 50 cm squares were separated into two groups: quartz/quartzite or non-quartz. The number of jasper flakes were also noted.

All lithics were also assessed as to their completeness. Fragmentary artifacts were grouped into one of three longitudinal classes (proximal, medial, distal). Lateral completeness was also considered for all large or specialized objects. In this classification, lithics were grouped into one of five non-exclusive categories; whole, left or right split, and left or right broken. The missing segment was noted while looking at the interior of the incomplete flake with the platform at the top. Cores were not subject to either measure of completeness as "wholeness" is difficult to quantify on these objects. Unbroken artifacts transformed by intentional retouch were considered complete objects. For purposes of analysis, a single measure of breakage was calculated; artifacts were judged to be whole, broken, or split. The few artifacts that were both broken and split were included only with split objects (n=29).

All debitage from excavation and screen bags was divided into three classes: complete flakes, broken flakes, or shatter. Shatter, or small chunks, are defined as lithics with no definable single interior surface (Sullivan and Rozen 1985, Baumler and

Downum 1989). Each grouping of flakes was counted and weighed.

The exterior cortex for all artifacts except cores was also considered. For individually recorded flakes, tools, and chunks, the amount of exterior cortical cover was judged to fall into one of five groups: <10%, 10-40%, 40-60%, 60-90%, or >90%. An estimate of platform cortex was made for each artifact with a distinguishable platform. Replicability studies conducted by Fish (1978,1979) have shown that the estimation of cortex can be extremely subjective. In his study, "observations on cortex varied widely and discrepancies between any two observer sets was always greater than 30%" (Fish 1979:45). For this study, all estimations of cortical cover were made by the same observer to reduce observer discrepancy. Secondly, most observers make estimations at regular intervals such as 25%, 33% or 50%. For added precision, categories of exterior cortex in this analysis were created to span the most common fractional ranges rather than to break at them.

Cortical presence was also noted for each of the flakes from excavation and screen bags. Debitage was divided into two groups; cortical and non-cortical. In this aspect of analysis, artifacts with any cortical cover were considered cortical. While a great deal of resolution was lost in this classification, the flakes were judged to be too numerous and too fragmentary to describe more precisely. Flakes in each class were counted and weighed as a group.

The placement of cortex on the exterior surface was judged to be in a left, right or center position for any individually numbered artifacts with cortex. The lateral cortex position was recorded in a manner similar to Toth's (1985) data for the Lower and Middle Paleolithic. Looking at the exterior of a flake, cortex was judged to be primarily located on the left or right margin or in the center of the flake surface.

The angle of deviation was also recorded for each complete flake and tool. A similar measurement, described by Leach (1969, cited in Jelinek 1977a), reflects the degree of deviation of a flake from being symmetrical. The measurement used in this study is the complement to Leach's "angle of skew" which is taken with the bulbar surface of the flake face down. In this analysis, artifacts were placed upon a radial grid with their point of percussion face up at the vertex and the plane of their striking platform on the 0°-180° axis. The deviation or angle of the point farthest from the point of percussion was noted (0°-40° strong left; 40°-80° left; 80°-100° center; 100°-140° right; 140°-180° strong right).

Platform surface has been used to distinguish reduction stages and technological variation. Generally, a platform with fewer facets can be expected to have been produced earlier in a reduction sequence. As reduction and preparation continue, platforms become more faceted. Complex platforms can also indicate technological variation (i.e. Levallois and biface manufacture). The platforms of all flakes and tools were classified into one of eight categories. Each platform was judged to be unfaceted (plain, cortical or transverse), faceted (dihedral, straight facet or convex facet) or absent (removed, shattered or missing).

Every flake and tool was also classified by technique of production. These typological classes form a focal point in this analysis of the La Quina lithics. Products of specific core reduction or tool rejuvenation processes were distinguished. These data will help to detect technological patterns; stages and techniques of lithic reduction will be discerned. Many broken artifacts or tools with intensive retouch were unclassifiable.

Defining attributes for Levallois and disc-core (pseudo-Levallois) products were taken from Bordes' typology (1961). To Bordes, the only correct definition of a Levallois flake is a flake with a form predetermined by special core preparation. These flakes can be described as plano-convex, frequently with faceted platforms (often convex), several intersecting exterior flake scars, and an axis of percussion that equals the axis of the tool. These diagnostic attributes reflect the "tortoise-shell" core preparation for flake removal. Disc-core reduction characteristically produces triangular flakes with dihedral platforms whose long axis diverges widely from the axis of flaking. Disc-core flakes often have peaked, sinuous ridges on their exterior surface reflecting radial core preparation.

Definitions for tool retouch flake were inspired by Frison (1968). He described two types of flakes from scraper retouch. The first and most common type is struck from the lower, unmodified surface of the tool producing a flake with a thin, wide, plain platform and a heavily retouched exterior surface. Scraper retouch flakes are occasionally struck from the tool edge to remove a portion of the flat basal surface of the artifact. This second type of scraper retouch flake has its striking platform on the dulled working edge of the tool and is relatively unscarred on its exterior surface. A third form of scraper retouch flakes was recognized at La Quina. Several flakes were struck from the end of the tool's working edge, driving a long, triangular wedge of marginal faceting from the artifact. Denticulate retouch flakes are similar to scraper retouch flakes in overall technique and morphology, but the removed working edge of the tool is serrated or notched rather than straight.

One of the most commonly recognized and studied types of debitage is produced during the manufacture of bifaces (Bordes 1961, Jelinek 1966 , Frison 1968, Newcomer 1971, Ahler 1989b). A bifacial thinning flake exhibits a combination of several distinctive characteristics including a thin, curved cross-section; feathered lateral and distal terminations; multiple dorsal flake scars; a small, thin faceted platform; little or no exterior cortex; interior lipping of the platform; a relatively small bulb of percussion; and an expanding flake shape (Ahler 1989b). Because of these detailed characteristics, a number of partial bifacial thinning flakes could be identified. As in the classification of scraper and denticulate retouch flakes, bifacial retouch or thinning flakes can be considered products of manufacture as well as rejuvenation.

Kombewa flakes were also distinguished in this analysis. First used by W.E. Owen (1938) to describe a simple flake-core industry in Kenya, Kombewa flakes are generally unretouched.

The flakes have what appear to be two bulbs of percussion on opposing faces and no obvious exterior surface. The form of these flakes can be nearly rectangular with rounded corners to ovate. The juncture of the interior and exterior flake surfaces of a Kombewa flake often form a smooth, sharp, curved edge. The term "Janus flake" has also been used to describe artifacts with these attributes (Tixier 1963).

The placement of flakes and tools into classes of general morphology developed for this study proved to be extremely subjective. The observation required placement of the artifact into one of nine categories that are not mutually exclusive (normal, angular, long-flat, ovoid/round-flat, long-thin, long-thick, short-wide, ovoid/round, triangular). For analysis, these categories were regrouped to give an indication of flake shape and thickness. Although the classification is faulty, broad patterns of flake production are distinguishable from this data set. Emphasis on the production of different tool forms or different stages of manufacture appears to affect the overall morphology and angularity of an assemblage.

Decisions on the number and morphology of exterior flake scars also proved to be relatively subjective. Classification was divided into nine groups that were not exhaustive or mutually exclusive (1 scar, 1 scar with retouch, 2 scars, 2 scars with retouch, more than 3 scars, more than three scars with retouch, plain, cortical, cortical with retouch). The groups were designed to reflect stages and technological patterns of reduction. These data were also recombined into two separate analyses. Information on early/late stage manufacture was gathered from the number of exterior scars, while reduction intensity was recognized from the presence of flakes with retouch scars in relation to those without evidence of retouch.

A measurement of length, width and thickness was taken on every complete tool and flake. The length was measured from the point of percussion along the axis of percussion to the point farthest from the point of percussion. The width was measured at the midpoint of the length, perpendicular to the length. The thickness was measured perpendicular to both the length and the width at the midpoint of width. These measurements could only be made if the artifact was almost or fully complete. These metric observations were taken to reflect the original size of flakes, so tools with intensive retouch on their margins were not measured.

Finally, each tool and core was analyzed. Where possible each core was classified by technique (Levallois or disc-core). The majority of cores from La Quina can best be defined as "irregular and polyfaceted" (Issac 1968) or "formless cores" (Clark and Kleindienst 1974). Tools were classified using Bordes' typology as to their primary type and their secondary type.

Conclusion

In order to detect variation in reduction strategies at La Quina each of the flakes, tools, cores and chunks in this sample was analyzed in detail. The attributes were chosen to detect changes in the technique and stage of lithic reduction that exist between beds. Analysis of this variation will be used to discern changes in patterns of tool morphology, core production, and intensity of lithic reduction at La Quina.

CHAPTER V

LA QUINA LITHICS: INTRA-SITE VARIABILITY

Introduction

This chapter presents the data and its analysis for this lithic study at La Quina. The analysis focuses on variation between assemblages within the site. Each assemblage includes the stone artifacts from a single archaeologically defined bed. First, broad variation in major lithic artifact categories and raw material are examined by stratum. Second, the quantification of attributes such as flake and platform morphology and cortical cover are presented and discussed in relation to stages of reduction and indications of technological variation. Artifacts with evidence of distinctive production techniques (i.e. Levallois or disc-core technology) are also discussed. Next, the retouched artifacts are classified according to Bordes (1961) typology for Middle Paleolithic tools. The relative frequencies of these traditional tool types are noted and compared by bed. Patterns of tool manufacture and reduction are discerned through a classification of technological by-products (i.e. tool preparation and rejuvenation flakes). Finally, size, completeness and weight of the flakes, tools, and cores are investigated. Variation in the frequencies of these metric attributes at La Quina is compared to indicators of technological variation.

Artifact Class

Table 1 presents the frequencies of major lithic artifact classes for individually recorded artifacts. These data were collected on 6392 individual artifacts from 13 recognized beds. The proportion of flakes, tools, cores and chunks are generally similar for each bed at La Quina, but a few minor variations in these frequencies are apparent. Kendall's tau test shows a very high probability for association between all pairs of major artifact classes (p <.005). Thus there is a generally uniform distribution of all four categories. A comparison of cases shows four groups of beds indicated by partitioned G-Square: Group 1 (4B, 6A, 6A1, 6C, 7, 8); Group 2 (C, D, E); Group 3 (G, L) and Group 4 (6D, M). Within these sets of beds there are no significant differences in frequencies of artifact classes. Variation between these four groups accounts for approximately 81 per cent of total matrix differences. The first group distinguishes the upper beds (except 6D) from the middle and lower beds. These upper beds have the most even distributions of artifacts by class. The groups of middle and lower beds (Groups 2 and 3) have lower percentages of cores and chunks than Group 1. The limited number of chunks in the middle and particularly in the lower beds indicate that the range of lithic activities in these contexts are more restricted than in the upper beds. Beds C, D, and E differ from Beds G and L in their higher relative frequency of tools and lower frequency of flakes. Beds 6D and M do not differ significantly and are significantly different from the other beds at La Quina. The high relative frequencies of flakes shared by these two beds results from the fact that bifacial retouch flakes in Bed 6D were plentiful and easily recognized in the screen/excavation flake bags as were scraper retouch flakes in the collection for Bed M.

Table 2 presents counts and relative frequencies from the upper beds (4B-8) for artifact class by location. This material is divided into three areas: artifacts found close to the cliff face (Back = Squares O1004 and N1004), far away from the cliff (Front = Square K1006), or in between (Middle = Squares M1005, M1006, and L1005) (Fig. 6). Spatial differences in major artifact classes are not significant; much of the total matrix difference can be accounted for by variation between beds. Variation between Bed 6D and the other upper "midden" beds is greater than any locational difference within these strata.

Raw Material

Another broad perspective on the lithics from La Quina can be gained from analysis of raw material. A basic identification of raw material was noted for every flake at La Quina in the individual, bag, and column samples. The sample from the flake bags includes more than 10,000 small flakes collected from excavation and screening sacs. Table 3 presents the combined data for the 6392 individually recorded artifacts and the flakes from excavation and screen bags. Almost all of the material used at La Quina was flint. Although the use of quartz/quartzite varies over time, it remains consistently low and no other raw material comprises a significant part of the lithic assemblage. The incidence of quartz at La Quina is highest in Beds 4B and 8, and moderate in Beds 7, L and M. Relative frequencies of quartz artifacts are lowest in Bed 6D. High numbers of bifacial thinning flakes and flake fragments in Bed 6D exaggerate the relative frequency of flint objects in this assemblage.

A breakdown of quartz objects by artifact class in Table 4 suggests that retouched artifacts were rarely made of quartz. Although quartz tools may be difficult to recognize, an effort was made to inspect all quartz objects for retouch or use. Most of the quartz objects at La Quina are unretouched flakes and nearly half of the recovered quartz tools are unretouched hammerstones. The beds with the highest relative frequencies of quartz artifacts are also those that have yielded hammerstones, and many of these battered, fractured quartz cobbles may have been the source of unretouched flakes and chunks found at La Quina. These locally available cobbles could have been used to smash large animal bones for their marrow or in lithic production and reduction.

The individually recorded artifact sample from the upper beds was divided by location for raw material analysis. Table 5 presents the numbers and relative frequencies for flint, quartz and other raw materials by location. Although most variation relates to differences between strata, percentages of quartz objects are lowest farthest from the cliff face and generally highest in the middle.

The data on raw materials for the nineteen column samples are presented in Table 6. These data are less consistent with the larger La Quina sample. Flint artifacts dominate each sample, but the incidence of quartz shows no apparent patterning. Variation in these samples may be complicated by the small size of each column unit and the inclusion of extremely small

TABLE 1 - ARTIFACTS BY CLASS: COUNTS AND PERCENTAGES

BED	FLKS	TOOLS	CORES	CHUNKS	N	BED	FLKS	TOOLS	CORES	CHUNKS
4B	288	94	9	32	423	4B	68.09	22.22	2.13	7.57
6A	581	141	22	49	793	6A	73.27	17.78	2.77	6.18
6A1	321	97	16	24	458	6A1	70.09	21.18	3.49	5.24
6C	480	119	28	44	671	6C	71.54	17.73	4.17	6.56
6D	843	109	12	22	986	6D	85.50	11.05	1.22	2.23
7	174	49	5	20	248	7	70.16	19.76	2.02	8.06
8	773	195	22	57	1047	8	73.83	18.62	2.10	5.44
C	57	24	1	5	87	C	65.52	27.59	1.15	5.75
D	112	43	2	4	161	D	69.57	26.71	1.24	2.48
E	116	43	4	3	166	E	69.88	25.90	2.41	1.81
G	577	141	13	17	748	G	77.14	18.85	1.74	2.27
L	340	91	2	14	447	L	76.06	20.36	0.45	3.13
M	132	16	2	7	157	M	84.08	10.19	1.27	4.46

6392

TABLE 2 - ARTIFACTS BY CLASS BY LOCATION: COUNTS AND PERCENTAGES

	FRONT					MIDDLE					BACK				
BED	FLAKE	TOOL	CORE	CHUNK	N	FLAKE	TOOL	CORE	CHUNK	N	FLAKE	TOOL	CORE	CHUNK	N
4B						258	87	8	27	380	30	7	1	5	43
6A	133	27	4	7	171	79	23	1	12	115	368	91	17	30	506
6C	210	51	10	20	291	80	19	4	6	109	183	49	14	18	264
6D	369	49	6	4	428	108	16	1	8	133	365	44	5	10	424
7	77	18	2	1	98	51	20	2	16	89	46	11	1	3	61
8	225	29	2	13	269	171	79	7	15	272	376	87	13	29	505
N	1014	174	24	45	1257	747	244	23	84	1098	1368	289	51	95	1803

	FRONT				MIDDLE				BACK			
BED	FLAKE	TOOL	CORE	CHUNK	FLAKE	TOOL	CORE	CHUNK	FLAKE	TOOL	CORE	CHUNK
4B					67.89	22.89	2.11	7.11	69.77	16.28	2.33	11.63
6A	77.78	15.79	2.34	4.09	68.70	20.00	0.87	10.43	72.73	17.98	3.36	5.93
6C	72.16	17.53	3.44	6.87	73.39	17.43	3.67	5.50	69.32	18.56	5.30	6.82
6D	86.21	11.45	1.40	0.93	81.20	12.03	0.75	6.02	86.08	10.38	1.18	2.36
7	78.57	18.37	2.04	1.02	57.30	22.47	2.25	17.98	75.41	18.03	1.64	4.92
8	83.64	10.78	0.74	4.83	62.87	29.04	2.57	5.51	74.46	17.23	2.57	5.74
N	80.67	13.84	1.91	3.58	68.03	22.22	2.09	7.65	75.87	16.03	2.83	5.27

TABLE 3 - RAW MATERIAL: COUNTS AND PERCENTAGES - ARTIFACTS AND FLAKE BAGS

BED	FLINT	QUARTZ	OTHER	N	BED	FLINT	QUARTZ	OTHER
4B	830	110	2	942	4B	88.11	11.68	0.21
6A	2220	117	8	2345	6A	94.67	4.99	0.34
6A1	998	49	2	1049	6A1	95.14	4.67	0.19
6C	1474	47	8	1529	6C	96.40	3.07	0.52
6D	3557	81	6	3644	6D	97.61	2.22	0.16
7	855	57	4	916	7	93.34	6.22	0.44
8	2387	249	8	2644	8	90.28	9.42	0.30
C	463	21	0	484	C	95.66	4.34	0.00
D	991	30	0	1021	D	97.06	2.94	0.00
E	473	21	1	495	E	95.56	4.24	0.20
G	1480	69	3	1552	G	95.36	4.45	0.19
L	858	65	4	927	L	92.56	7.01	0.43
M	317	22	0	339	M	93.51	6.49	0.00

TABLE 4 - QUARTZ ARTIFACTS BY CLASS: COUNTS AND PERCENTAGES

BED	FLAKE	TOOL	CORE	CHUNK	N	FLAKE	TOOL	CORE	CHUNK
4B	36	2	0	9	47	76.60	4.26	0.00	19.15
6A	15	2	0	13	30	50.00	6.67	0.00	43.33
6A1	14	0	0	4	18	77.78	0.00	0.00	22.22
6C	4	1	0	5	10	40.00	10.00	0.00	50.00
6D	10	1	0	3	14	71.43	7.14	0.00	21.43
7	8	2	1	8	19	42.11	10.53	5.26	42.11
8	53	6	1	24	84	63.10	7.14	1.19	28.57
C	2	0	0	1	3	66.67	0.00	0.00	33.33
D	2	1	0	0	3	66.67	33.33	0.00	0.00
E	3	0	0	0	3	100.00	0.00	0.00	0.00
G	17	1	0	1	19	89.47	5.26	0.00	5.26
L	11	0	0	7	18	61.11	0.00	0.00	38.89
M	5	2	0	2	9	55.56	22.22	0.00	22.22

QUARTZ TOOLS

BED		
	4B	HAMMERSTONE (1)
	6A	NOTCH (2)
	6C	DENT (1)
	6D	NOTCH (1)
	7	DENT (1)
		IRR RET (1)
	8	HAMMERSTONE (4)
		DENT (1)
		LT RET (1)
	D	LT RET (1)
	G	HAMMERSTONE (1)
	M	HAMMERSTONE (1)
		SCRAPER (1)

TABLE 5 - RAW MATERIAL BY LOCATION: COUNTS AND PERCENTAGES

	FRONT				MIDDLE				BACK			
BED	FLINT	QUARTZ	OTHER	N	FLINT	QUARTZ	OTHER	N	FLINT	QUARTZ	OTHER	N
4B					332	46	2	380	41	2	0	43
6A	167	4	0	171	108	5	2	115	480	23	3	506
6C	283	6	2	291	106	0	3	109	257	4	3	264
6D	423	3	2	428	126	3	4	133	416	8	0	424
7	93	5	0	98	76	9	4	89	56	5	0	61
8	250	16	3	269	242	29	1	272	461	40	4	505

	FRONT			MIDDLE			BACK		
BED	FLINT	QUARTZ	OTHER	FLINT	QUARTZ	OTHER	FLINT	QUARTZ	OTHER
4B				87.37	12.11	0.53	95.35	4.65	0.00
6A	97.66	2.34	0.00	93.91	4.35	1.74	94.86	4.55	0.59
6C	97.25	2.06	0.69	97.25	0.00	2.75	97.35	1.52	1.14
6D	98.83	0.70	0.47	94.74	2.26	3.01	98.11	1.89	0.00
7	94.90	5.10	0.00	85.39	10.11	4.49	91.80	8.20	0.00
8	92.94	5.95	1.12	88.97	10.66	0.37	91.29	7.92	0.79

TABLE 6 - RAW MATERIAL: COUNTS AND PERCENTAGES - COLUMN SAMPLES

		FLINT	QUARTZ	OTHER	N			FLINT	QUARTZ	OTHER
L1005	6A	17	1	0	18	L1005	6A	94.44	5.56	0.00
	6C	195	24	0	219		6C	89.04	10.96	0.00
	6D	310	14	0	324		6D	95.68	4.32	0.00
	8	234	32	2	268		8	87.31	11.94	0.75
M1005	6A	47	5	1	53	M1005	6A	88.68	9.43	1.89
		46	6	0	52			88.46	11.54	0.00
	6C	59	2	0	61		6C	96.72	3.28	0.00
		68	7	1	76			89.47	9.21	1.32
	6D	145	2	0	147		6D	98.64	1.36	0.00
		151	15	0	166			90.96	9.04	0.00
	8	214	9	0	223		8	95.96	4.04	0.00
		336	42	1	379			88.65	11.08	0.26
N1004	6A	25	3	0	28	N1004	6A	89.29	10.71	0.00
	6C	36	0	0	36		6C	100.00	0.00	0.00
	6D	174	7	0	181		6D	96.13	3.87	0.00
H1005	G	64	1	0	65	H1005	G	98.46	1.54	0.00
		65	10	0	75			86.67	13.33	0.00
F1006	M	22	0	0	22	F1006	M	100.00	0.00	0.00
		14	1	0	15			93.33	6.67	0.00

TABLE 7 - CORTEX ON ARTIFACTS: COUNTS, RELATIVE & CUMULATIVE FREQUENCIES

BED	<10%	10-40%	40-60%	60-90%	>90%	N
4B	255	93	29	17	18	412
6A	499	144	40	59	29	771
6A1	286	96	20	22	18	442
6C	391	144	37	53	16	641
6D	826	85	22	31	9	973
7	177	33	11	13	9	243
8	691	183	56	51	43	1024
C	69	6	2	4	5	86
D	119	21	10	6	3	159
E	117	25	6	5	9	162
G	518	145	27	24	20	734
L	321	66	16	23	19	445
M	116	20	10	6	3	155

BED	>10%	10-40%	40-60%	60-90%	>90%	BED	>10%	10-40%	40-60%	60-90%	>90%
4B	61.89	22.57	7.04	4.13	4.37	4B	4.37	8.50	15.53	38.11	100.00
6A	64.72	18.68	5.19	7.65	3.76	6A	3.76	11.41	16.60	35.28	100.00
6A1	64.71	21.72	4.52	4.98	4.07	6A1	4.07	9.05	13.57	35.29	100.00
6C	61.00	22.46	5.77	8.27	2.50	6C	2.50	10.76	16.54	39.00	100.00
6D	84.89	8.74	2.26	3.19	0.92	6D	0.92	4.11	6.37	15.11	100.00
7	72.84	13.58	4.53	5.35	3.70	7	3.70	9.05	13.58	27.16	100.00
8	67.48	17.87	5.47	4.98	4.20	8	4.20	9.18	14.65	32.52	100.00
C	80.23	6.98	2.33	4.65	5.81	C	5.81	10.47	12.79	19.77	100.00
D	74.84	13.21	6.29	3.77	1.89	D	1.89	5.66	11.95	25.16	100.00
E	72.22	15.43	3.70	3.09	5.56	E	5.56	8.64	12.35	27.78	100.00
G	70.57	19.75	3.68	3.27	2.72	G	2.72	5.99	9.67	29.43	100.00
L	72.13	14.83	3.60	5.17	4.27	L	4.27	9.44	13.03	27.87	100.00
M	74.84	12.90	6.45	3.87	1.94	M	1.94	5.81	12.26	25.16	100.00

(>1 mm) lithic pieces. Some of these small quartz pieces may represent limestone inclusions rather than culturally imported material.

REDUCTION STAGES

Having considered the basic artifact groups and raw material used at La Quina, the morphology of flakes and flake tools can be considered. The amount of cortex and number of scars on the exterior surface of a flake can be used to examine reduction processes. The earliest stages of reduction on a flint nodule will produce cortical flakes with few scars. As reduction continues, flakes will have less cortex and more exterior flake scars. Unfortunately, cortex removal is not a linear process. The removal of cortex can be rapid and complete at an early stage of manufacture, but cortex can also be present throughout the reduction process (Maudlin and Amick 1989). In this study, cortex position and angle of deviation for each flake are also considered along with general flake form and thickness. These classifications are used as ancillary descriptive information to compare of flake morphology between strata. Finally, exterior scar number and form is considered in relation to reduction stages and technique.

Cortex

Table 7 shows the primary data on cortex for flakes and tools at La Quina from the individual artifact sample. The number and relative frequencies of each class of cortex are presented along with a table of the same data in cumulative fashion. The amount and frequency of cortical cover does not vary widely between beds at La Quina. More flakes with greater cortical cover are present in the upper beds than in the lower ones, but Beds 6D and C can be distinguished from all other beds. The frequency of flakes with any cortex in Bed 6D is only 15 per cent - about half of the frequency found in most of the other assemblages at La Quina. The difference may be due to the high numbers of non-cortical biface retouch flakes found in this bed. A relatively low percentage (20%) of cortical flakes is also present in Bed C may be attributed to intensive use of this slope material as was also suggested by the high percentage of tools in this assemblage.

The data on cortex again suggest that differences between the upper and lower beds can account for much of the variability recognized at La Quina. This variability may be related to the broader spectrum of lithic activity recognized in the upper beds, especially early stage lithic reduction. Unique patterns of technology and reduction in Bed 6D distinguish this assemblage from all other samples. Four groups of beds are indicated by partitioned G-Square analysis (Beds 4B-6C, 7-C, E-M, 6D/D). Variation between these groups accounts for three-quarters (74%) of the total G-Square matrix differences.

Data on cortex for the flake bags are presented in Table 8 and data for the column samples are presented in Table 9. Although flakes with any cortex at all were classified as cortical, these smaller flakes have less tendency to be cortical than the larger artifacts (where cortical > 10%). As with the individually recorded data, the lowest percentage of flakes with cortex is found in Bed 6D and the highest percentage is found

in Bed 6C. However, differences between the upper and lower beds are not seen in these samples. All beds except C have lower percentages of small cortical flakes than large individually recorded ones, but the differences are most exaggerated in the upper beds. Beds 4B and 6A1 have respectively 17 per cent and 18 per cent more large cortical flakes than small ones. The lower number of large cortical artifacts and higher number of small cortical flakes in Bed C may again be a reflection of its high retouched tool component or the small sample size of this assemblage.

The data from the column samples in Table 9 replicate the information from the individually recorded artifact sample. The column samples from Bed 6C have the highest percentage of cortical flakes while the samples from Bed 6D have the lowest numbers of cortical flakes. Flakes in the Beds G and M samples also have relatively low frequencies of cortical flakes. The occurrence of cortical flakes appears to be slightly elevated closest to the cliff face in N1004, but this sample is too small for conclusive interpretation.

Table 10 presents the data for cortex by location for the individually recorded artifacts in the upper beds. These frequencies confirm that, in general, more cortical flakes are found at the back of the site. This pattern is particularly pronounced in Beds 7 and 8. The frequency of cortical flakes in Bed 6D remains consistently low in all areas.

Cortex Position

Table 11 presents the data on the frequencies for position of cortex on the exterior surface of individually recorded flakes and tools. These data do little to reveal any variation in technology or manufacture. The position of cortex on tools and flakes in most beds is equally divided between the three categories: left, right and center. On the other hand, Beds 6C and 6D have higher proportions of left cortical flakes (10 % more) while Beds D and G have an equally higher proportion of flakes with cortex on their right side.

Angle of Deviation

The data presented in Table 12 do not reveal any strong patterns of variation in the angle of deviation. Roughly two-thirds of all flakes have their longest point centered directly below their point of percussion. The remaining one-third of the flakes are equally split between left- and right-deviated. The uppermost beds at La Quina (Beds 4B through 6D) show a slight tendency for greater numbers of left- than right-deviated flakes. At an extreme, Bed 6A1 has nearly two times as many left-deviated flakes as right-deviated. Selection for right-deviated flakes during the excavation and re-excavation of materials from the pit may explain these numbers. The increased relative frequency of "central" flakes in Bed 6D can be related to the tendency for bifacial retouch flakes to be long and straight. The dominance of left-deviated flakes in the upper beds is reversed from Bed 7 down (with the exception of Bed E). These data again suggest a basic difference between the upper and lower beds at La Quina. Again, the meaning of this variation is unclear, but comparisons between the data on cortex position and deviation show a tendency to left deviatio/cortex in the upper strata and

TABLE 8 - CORTEX: FLAKE BAGS (FLINT ONLY) - COUNTS AND PERCENTAGES

BED	CORTICAL	NON-CORT	N	CORTICAL	NON-CORT
4B	97	360	457	21.23	78.77
6A	342	1123	1465	23.34	76.66
6A1	93	447	540	17.22	82.78
6C	245	576	821	29.84	70.16
6D	205	2386	2591	7.91	92.09
7	111	319	430	25.81	74.19
8	269	1164	1433	18.77	81.23
C	99	280	379	26.12	73.88
D	163	806	969	16.82	83.18
E	67	244	311	21.54	78.46
G	151	603	754	20.03	79.97
L	104	329	433	24.02	75.98
M	37	132	169	21.89	78.11

TABLE 9 - CORTEX: COLUMN SAMPLES - COUNTS AND PERCENTAGES

SQ BED	CORTICAL	NON-CORT	N	CORTICAL	NON-CORT
L1005 6A	0	18	18	0.00	100.00
6C	23	196	219	10.50	89.50
6D	7	37	324	2.16	97.84
8	22	246	268	8.21	91.79
M1005 6A	6	47	53	11.32	88.68
	1	51	52	1.92	98.08
6C	3	58	61	4.92	95.08
	9	67	76	11.84	88.16
6D	2	145	147	1.36	98.64
8	7	216	223	3.14	96.86
	15	34	379	3.96	96.04
N1004 6A	2	26	28	7.14	92.86
6C	6	30	36	16.67	83.33
6D	3	178	181	1.66	98.34
	7	159	166	4.22	95.78
H1005 G	0	65	65	0.00	100.00
	6	69	75	8.00	92.00
F1006 M	1	21	22	4.55	95.45
	0	15	5	0.00	0.00

TABLE 10 - CORTEX BY LOCATION: COUNTS AND PERCENTAGES

	FRONT				MIDDLE				BACK		
BED	CORT	NCORT	N		CORT	NCORT	N		CORT	NCORT	N
4B					142	230	372		17	25	42
6A	57	110	167		33	81	114		182	307	489
6C	109	172	281		41	64	105		101	149	250
6D	64	358	422		23	109	132		62	357	419
7	15	81	96		28	59	87		37	23	60
8	109	158	267		94	171	265		327	165	492
N	354	879	1233		361	714	1075		726	1026	1752

	FRONT			MIDDLE			BACK	
BED	CORT	NCORT		CORT	NCORT		CORT	NCORT
4B				38.17	61.83		40.48	59.52
6A	34.13	65.87		28.95	71.05		37.22	62.78
6C	38.79	61.21		39.05	60.95		40.40	59.60
6D	15.17	84.83		17.42	82.58		14.80	85.20
7	15.63	84.38		32.18	67.82		61.67	38.33
8	40.82	59.18		35.47	64.53		66.46	33.54
N	28.71	71.29		33.58	66.42		41.44	58.56

TABLE 11 - CORTEX POSITION: COUNTS AND PERCENTAGES

BED	LEFT	CENTER	RIGHT	N		LEFT	CENTER	RIGHT
4B	55	43	57	155		35.48	27.74	36.77
6A	92	90	91	273		33.70	32.97	33.33
6A1	53	54	49	156		33.97	34.62	31.41
6C	97	79	70	246		39.43	32.11	28.46
6D	59	52	44	155		38.06	33.55	28.39
7	20	32	16	68		29.41	47.06	23.53
8	107	136	115	358		29.89	37.99	32.12
C	4	11	3	18		22.22	61.11	16.67
D	12	12	17	41		29.27	29.27	41.46
E	17	20	14	51		33.33	39.22	27.45
G	66	66	85	217		30.41	30.41	39.17
L	48	50	37	135		35.56	37.04	27.41
M	12	17	11	40		30.00	42.50	27.50
N	642	662	609	1913		33.56	34.61	31.83

TABLE 12 - ANGLE OF DEVIATION: COUNTS AND PERCENTAGES

BED	STRONG LEFT	LEFT	CENTER	RIGHT	STRONG RIGHT	N	STRONG LEFT	LEFT	CENTER	RIGHT	STRONG RIGHT
4B	1	68	187	64	1	321	0.31	21.18	58.26	19.94	0.31
6A	9	112	360	114	4	599	1.50	18.70	60.10	19.03	0.67
6A1	4	73	179	39	1	296	1.35	24.66	60.47	13.18	0.34
6C	3	106	306	106	2	523	0.57	20.27	58.51	20.27	0.38
6D	2	95	464	88	4	653	0.31	14.55	71.06	13.48	0.61
7	2	34	106	35	3	180	1.11	18.89	58.89	19.44	1.67
8	1	142	491	144	11	789	0.13	18.00	62.23	18.25	1.39
C	0	9	41	13	0	63	0.00	14.29	65.08	20.63	0.00
D	0	16	72	22	2	112	0.00	14.29	64.29	19.64	1.79
E	0	27	64	22	0	113	0.00	23.89	56.64	19.47	0.00
G	5	91	308	114	7	525	0.95	17.33	58.67	21.71	1.30
L	3	55	204	73	1	336	0.89	16.37	60.71	21.73	0.30
M	1	21	71	31	2	126	0.79	16.67	56.35	24.60	1.59
N	31	849	2853	865	38	4636					

and right deviation/cortex in the lower deposits. A slight overall trend over time for left cortical flakes and right-deviated flakes should also be noted.

Flake Morphology
Nine categories of flake shape were defined for flakes and flake tools in the La Quina sample. The classification comprises a general morphological description for each individually recorded flake and tool. The nine morphological groups were combined in two different ways to reflect flake shape and thickness. Although this classification is subjective, an impression of variation in flake form can be gained from Table 13. Variation in relative thickness of flakes between beds is shown in Table 14.

Table 13 reveals that Beds L and M have high relative frequencies of long and ovoid/round flakes, while Beds 7 through E are characterized by more short-wide and nondescript "average" flakes. Beds 4B, 6A and 6C have high numbers of angular and average flakes, but Beds 6A1 and G have few average or angular flakes. The low number of average flakes in Bed 6A1 may reflect special attention paid to these lithics. However, these data might also reflect culling of these "average" flakes from the 6A1 material during repeated episodes of pit excavation and filling.

These general changes in flake shape over time can be related to variation in lithic reduction. At the base of the La Quina sequence (Beds L and M) and in Bed 6D, activities appear to have centered on the reduction of even-edged tools with little evidence of early stage manufacture or reduction. In the case of Bed 6D, however, quantities of bifacial retouch flakes may mask evidence for other lithic activities. In the middle group of beds (7-E), a broader spectrum of flake forms are found. At the top of the sequence (Beds 4B, 6A and 6C), the assemblages are characterized by many angular and unspecialized flakes. Flake morphology confirms that these beds contain more products of early stage reduction than the lower beds. These technological differences are also indicated by distance coefficient analysis. Ovoid/round and long flakes show a very close relationship, as do triangular and short-wide flakes, and average and angular flakes. In contrast, ovoid/round and long flakes are each distant from average and angular shaped flakes.

The data in Table 14 present a consideration of overall thickness for each flake and flake tool in the individually recorded artifact sample. Analysis of these data indicate groupings similar to those recognized in the analysis of flake shape. The two lowest beds (L and M) are alike in the prevalence of relatively thin flakes. Bed 6D is similar to these two beds, but has a predominance of very thin, or flat flakes (40 %). The flakes from the middle beds (Beds 6A1, 7-G) are neither extremely thin nor extremely thick. The remaining upper beds at La Quina (Beds 4B, 6A and 6C) contain thick, angular flakes and limited numbers of thin or flat flakes. These impressions of angularity will be examined less subjectively in analyses of the metric data from La Quina.

Exterior Flake Scars
The number of the exterior flake scars for each individually

recorded flake and tool is shown in Table 15. At the extremes of variability, high numbers of flakes with three or more flake scars in Bed 6D (66%) can be contrasted with relatively low frequencies for such flakes in Bed 6A (32%). Bed 4B (49%), Bed 7 (51%), and Bed C (47%) also have relatively high frequencies of flakes with more than three exterior flake scars. Although some indication of patterning can be seen in this analysis, the range of variation for this classification is not great enough to reflect strong differences between all beds at La Quina.

Platform Morphology: Cortex
In the same ways that cortex and scar counts can be related to reduction processes, the amount of cortex and the facets on the platform of a flake can be related to reduction strategies. Generally, flakes produced in later stages of manufacture will have less cortex on their platform and more flake scars than flakes produced during primary stages of reduction. Table 16 presents the data on platform cortex. The number of flakes with any platform cortex (<10%) is low for most of the beds at La Quina.

The lowest frequencies of cortex on flake platforms are found in Bed 6D. Only 5 per cent of the flakes in this assemblage have any cortex on their platforms. This frequency can again be related to production of numerous, non-cortical flakes in the process of biface reduction. In contrast, Bed 4B is notable for its high frequency of early stage reduction products. Nearly a quarter (22%) of the flakes in Bed 4B have some cortex on their platform and 12 per cent of the flakes in Bed 4B have fully cortical platforms. Between these two extremes, the frequencies for platform cortex from other beds range between 7 and 14 per cent. Beds 6A1, 6D, C, G and M have relatively few flakes with cortex on their platforms (5-8%). A second group (Beds 6A, 6C, 7, 8, D, E and L) is characterized by higher frequencies of cortex on their platforms (10-14%).

Platform Surface
The number and direction of flake scars on the platform of a tool or flake can also be related to manufacture technique. While simple, unfaceted platforms (plain or transverse) are most often related to early or unpatterned reduction, multi-faceted platforms are most commonly achieved during patterned reduction of cores or bifaces. Table 17 presents data on platform morphology of individually recorded flakes and tools. The frequencies are given first by individual class and then by group (unfaceted or faceted). Unfaceted platforms are defined as having a single flake scar in any direction, while faceted platforms exhibit multiple flake scars. All beds except 6D at La Quina are dominated by flakes with unfaceted platforms. Bed 6D has almost twice as many flakes with faceted platforms (30%) as any other bed. Intermediate frequencies of faceted platforms are found in Beds 7 and 8. Directional change between the upper and lower beds at La Quina can again be noted. There is a trend for increased numbers of flakes with multi-faceted platforms from the base of the site through Bed 6D. Beds 6C-4B have relatively high frequencies of unfaceted platforms.

Data on other types of platforms suggest that removed and

TABLE 13 - FLAKE SHAPE: COUNTS AND PERCENTAGES

BED	ANGULAR	SH-WIDE	LONG	AVG	OVOID/RD	ANGULAR	N
4B	42	57	33	109	71	27	339
6A	117	159	60	176	69	57	638
6A1	29	99	65	6	77	36	312
6C	128	95	73	128	85	33	542
6D	51	87	179	75	264	28	684
7	18	39	35	33	46	11	182
8	97	195	132	183	183	42	832
C	9	18	10	14	10	6	67
D	18	25	16	18	33	6	116
E	18	25	23	18	20	10	114
G	40	130	101	34	164	60	529
L	23	42	60	48	133	28	334
M	9	20	25	15	47	9	125

BED	ANGULAR	SH-WIDE	LONG	AVG	OVOID/RD	ANGULAR
4B	12.39	16.81	9.73	32.15	20.94	7.96
6A	18.34	24.92	9.40	27.59	10.82	8.93
6A1	9.29	31.73	20.83	1.92	24.68	11.54
6C	23.62	17.53	13.47	23.62	15.68	6.09
6D	7.46	12.72	26.17	10.96	38.60	4.09
7	9.89	21.43	19.23	18.13	25.27	6.04
8	11.66	23.44	15.87	22.00	22.00	5.05
C	13.43	26.87	14.93	20.90	14.93	8.96
D	15.52	21.55	13.79	15.52	28.45	5.17
E	15.79	21.93	20.18	15.79	17.54	8.77
G	7.56	24.57	19.09	6.43	31.00	11.34
L	6.89	12.57	17.96	14.37	39.82	8.38
M	7.20	16.00	20.00	12.00	37.60	7.20

TABLE 14 - FLAKE THICKNESS: COUNTS AND PERCENTAGES

BED	ANGULAR	WIDE	THICK	AVG	THIN	FLAT	N
4B	42	57	25	203	8	4	339
6A	117	159	45	301	11	5	638
6A1	29	99	37	117	16	14	312
6C	128	95	57	242	15	5	542
6D	51	87	27	202	45	272	684
7	18	39	13	76	16	20	182
8	97	195	59	379	67	35	832
C	9	18	4	30	5	1	67
D	18	25	7	52	9	5	116
E	18	25	10	42	11	8	114
G	40	130	44	207	53	55	529
L	23	42	31	166	24	48	334
M	9	20	8	46	14	28	125

BED	ANGULAR	WIDE	THICK	AVG	THIN	FLAT
4B	12.39	16.81	7.37	59.88	2.36	1.18
6A	18.34	24.92	7.05	47.18	1.72	0.78
6A1	9.29	31.73	11.86	37.50	5.13	4.49
6C	23.62	17.53	10.52	44.65	2.77	0.92
6D	7.46	12.72	3.95	29.53	6.58	39.77
7	9.89	21.43	7.14	41.76	8.79	10.99
8	11.66	23.44	7.09	45.55	8.05	4.21
C	13.43	26.87	5.97	44.78	7.46	1.49
D	15.52	21.55	6.03	44.83	7.76	4.31
E	15.79	21.93	8.77	36.84	9.65	7.02
G	7.56	24.57	8.32	39.13	10.02	10.40
L	6.89	12.57	9.28	49.70	7.19	14.37
M	7.20	16.00	6.40	36.80	11.20	22.40

TABLE 15 - FLAKE SCARS: COUNTS AND PERCENTAGES

BED	CORT	PLAIN/ 1 SCAR	2 SCARS	3+ SCARS	N	CORT	PLAIN/ 1 SCAR	2 SCARS	3+ SCARS
4B	38	83	56	171	348	10.92	23.85	16.09	49.14
6A	70	230	157	213	670	10.45	34.33	23.43	31.79
6A1	40	109	81	189	419	9.55	26.01	19.33	45.11
6C	55	179	114	240	588	9.35	30.44	19.39	40.82
6D	28	138	141	603	910	3.08	15.16	15.49	66.26
7	11	51	45	111	218	5.05	23.39	20.64	50.92
8	89	288	198	377	952	9.35	30.25	20.80	39.60
C	8	14	19	37	78	10.26	17.95	24.36	47.44
D	8	35	27	62	132	6.06	26.52	20.45	46.97
E	16	48	38	56	158	10.13	30.38	24.05	35.44
G	53	235	115	301	704	7.53	33.38	16.34	42.76
L	39	123	100	163	425	9.18	28.94	23.53	38.35
M	6	53	34	53	146	4.11	36.30	23.29	36.30

TABLE 16 - PLATFORM CORTEX: COUNTS, RELATIVE & CUMULATIVE FREQUENCIES

BED	> 90%	90-50%	50-10%	< 10%	N
4B	42	6	27	271	346
6A	27	16	29	557	629
6A1	14	4	9	319	346
6C	17	7	27	482	533
6D	20	5	13	730	768
7	14	0	10	154	178
8	60	10	16	737	823
C	2	2	0	61	65
D	6	1	4	119	130
E	9	3	7	116	135
G	31	5	12	579	627
L	27	2	12	346	387
M	5	0	4	128	137

BED	> 90%	90-50%	50-10%	< 10%	BED	> 90%	> 50%	> 10%	> 0%
4B	12.14	1.73	7.80	78.32	4B	12.14	13.87	21.68	100.00
6A	4.29	2.54	4.61	88.55	6A	4.29	6.84	11.45	100.00
6A1	4.05	1.16	2.60	92.20	6A1	4.05	5.20	7.80	100.00
6C	3.19	1.31	5.07	90.43	6C	3.19	4.50	9.57	100.00
6D	2.60	0.65	1.69	95.05	6D	2.60	3.26	4.95	100.00
7	7.87	0.00	5.62	86.52	7	7.87	7.87	13.48	100.00
8	7.29	1.22	1.94	89.55	8	7.29	8.51	10.45	100.00
C	3.08	3.08	0.00	93.85	C	3.08	6.15	6.15	100.00
D	4.62	0.77	3.08	91.54	D	4.62	5.38	8.46	100.00
E	6.67	2.22	5.19	85.93	E	6.67	8.89	14.07	100.00
G	4.94	0.80	1.91	92.34	G	4.94	5.74	7.66	100.00
L	6.98	0.52	3.10	89.41	L	6.98	7.49	10.59	100.00
M	3.65	0.00	2.92	93.43	M	3.65	3.65	6.57	100.00

TABLE 17 - PLATFORM SURFACE: COUNTS AND PERCENTAGES

BED	PLAIN	TVSE	DIHEDR	STRGHT FACET	CONVEX FACET	REMVD	SHATRD	MISNG	N
4B	298	10	9	2	3	5	3	45	375
6A	540	19	31	18	6	11	10	81	716
6A1	304	9	13	13	2	1	2	74	418
6C	455	17	24	16	6	6	9	65	598
6D	441	7	18	258	11	10	24	178	947
7	125	1	11	22	4	5	8	46	222
8	627	21	42	65	30	18	23	129	955
C	51	4	4	3	1	2	1	15	81
D	109	1	5	7	1	1	3	27	154
E	114	4	3	4	1	2	9	22	159
G	553	17	17	11	2	4	27	86	717
L	334	4	5	14	3	12	26	31	429
M	124	0	0	2	0	3	10	9	148

BED	PLAIN	TVSE	DIHEDR	STRGHT FACET	CONVEX FACET	REMVD	SHATRD	MISNG
4B	79.47	2.67	2.40	0.53	0.80	1.33	0.80	12.00
6A	75.42	2.65	4.33	2.51	0.84	1.54	1.40	11.31
6A1	72.73	2.15	3.11	3.11	0.48	0.24	0.48	17.70
6C	76.09	2.84	4.01	2.68	1.00	1.00	1.51	10.87
6D	46.57	0.74	1.90	27.24	1.16	1.06	2.53	18.80
7	56.31	0.45	4.95	9.91	1.80	2.25	3.60	20.72
8	65.65	2.20	4.40	6.81	3.14	1.88	2.41	13.51
C	62.96	4.94	4.94	3.70	1.23	2.47	1.23	18.52
D	70.78	0.65	3.25	4.55	0.65	0.65	1.95	17.53
E	71.70	2.52	1.89	2.52	0.63	1.26	5.66	13.84
G	77.13	2.37	2.37	1.53	0.28	0.56	3.77	11.99
L	77.86	0.93	1.17	3.26	0.70	2.80	6.06	7.23
M	83.78	0.00	0.00	1.35	0.00	2.03	6.76	6.08

BED	UN-FACETD	FACETD	ABSENT	UN-FACETD	FACETD	ABSENT	N
4B	308	14	53	82.13	3.73	14.13	375
6A	559	55	102	78.07	7.68	14.25	716
6A1	313	28	77	74.88	6.70	18.42	418
6C	472	46	80	78.93	7.69	13.38	598
6D	448	287	212	47.31	30.31	22.39	947
7	126	37	59	56.76	16.67	26.58	222
8	648	137	170	67.85	14.35	17.80	955
C	55	8	18	67.90	9.88	22.22	81
D	110	13	31	71.43	8.44	20.13	154
E	118	8	33	74.21	5.03	20.75	159
G	570	30	117	79.50	4.18	16.32	717
L	338	22	69	78.79	5.13	16.08	429
M	124	2	22	83.78	1.35	14.86	148

shattered platforms are strongly associated, but their distribution is not significantly similar to that of flakes with missing platforms. Flakes with missing platforms show a much stronger association with flakes that have platforms than with flakes with removed or shattered platforms. The frequencies for missing platforms vary more widely (21-6%) between beds than those of removed or shattered platforms (0-7%). There is a slight trend for fewer removed or shattered platforms over time. More flakes without platforms are found in the upper-middle and early upper strata. Factors of breakage such as flake thickness and depositional context may have been responsible for the elevated frequencies of missing platforms in Beds 6D, 7, and C. An emphasis on early stage reduction in the upper beds may have resulted in fewer removed or shattered platforms in these contexts.

Technology: Reduction Techniques
Where possible, the technological pattern of core reduction and flake production were identified on flakes, tools and cores in the sample of 6392 artifacts. Disc-core and Levallois by-products are used as indicators of such reduction techniques. The disc-core and Levallois classes in the La Quina assemblages are largely comprised of unretouched flakes from cores prepared using one of these techniques. Table 18 shows the data for products of patterned core reduction. Table 19 gives counts and frequencies for cores and the technique used to produce them. Production of Kombewa flakes was distinguished as an additional potential technological pattern and these data are presented in Table 20.

As Table 18 shows, very little evidence of the Levallois technique was found at La Quina. The use of Levallois preparation and reduction can only be recognized in Bed 8. Fourteen identifiable Levallois flakes comprise only 1 per cent of the artifacts in the sample, and a flake from the pit structure (Bed 6A1) was most probably displaced by post-depositional disturbance. This flake and a core from Bed 7 represent the only other evidence of Levallois technique in the upper and middle beds. The high numbers of flakes with multi-faceted platforms in Bed 8 may be related to the use of Levallois technique in this context. The high frequencies of such flakes in Bed 7 and the presence of the Levallois core in this collection suggest that the Bed 7 industry represents a continuation of that of Bed 8. A single flake of Levallois technique was identified in Bed L.

Evidence of disc-core production is more abundant than that of Levallois. All beds at La Quina had at least a few identifiable flakes or cores of disc-core technique. Most of the recognizable by-products are unretouched flakes and very small cores. Beds 6C and 6A have the highest frequencies of disc-core products with 14 per cent and 10 per cent respectively. An intermediate level of disc-core products in Bed 6A1 (7%) may again reflect mixing of parent beds. Few examples of disc-core reduction were found in the lowest beds (1% each in G, L and M), and confirm earlier indications that the lithic assemblages from these lower beds are different from those of the upper beds, particularly in relation to patterned core reduction.

Of the 138 cores found in the La Quina sample, 94 (or 68%) have a radial, angular scar pattern typical of disc-core reduction (Table 19). It is possible that more disc-core and Levallois core preparation was practiced at La Quina than is evident from these intensively utilized artifacts. Many cores are so heavily reduced and the flakes so frequently altered by retouch and breakage that identification of specific reduction techniques is impossible. Reduction technique for these formless, irregular cores was categorized as "other". Cores from the lower levels appear to be less reduced and less patterned in their reduction.

Kombewa flakes (Owen 1938) were considered in this classification as a technological means to produce sharp, even-edged flakes. As the relative frequencies of these flakes do not vary markedly through the sequence at La Quina, the form cannot be shown to reflect a distinct cultural pattern (Table 20).

RETOUCHED ARTIFACTS
Tool Typology
The classification of tools for this study is presented in Tables 21, 22, and 23. Each artifact with recognizable intentional retouch was classified according to Bordes' typology (1961) and data on this classification are presented in Tables 21 and 22. The frequency of denticulates, notched pieces, scrapers and bifaces are given in Table 23. Flint tools classified on Table 23 are lumped together into the fifth column, "other" tools on Table 23.

Several of the lowest beds at La Quina are characterized by high percentages of scrapers. Although the sample of tools from Bed M is very small, the frequencies of tool types are similar to the larger samples from Beds G and L. The tool assemblages from Beds G, L, and M at La Quina are comprised respectively of 57 per cent, 71 per cent and 75 per cent scrapers. High frequencies of scrapers characterize Bordes' Quina Mousterian (Bordes 1966, Bordes and de Sonneville-Bordes 1970). This variant is also distinguished by the presence of several special kinds of scrapers, all of which can be found at La Quina. The first of these special scraper types, "Quina" scrapers, was initially recognized by Henri-Martin at this site. Quina scrapers are usually made on thick flakes with a convex working edge and invasive scalar retouch. Intensive reuse of even-edged tools also results in the production of limaces and bifacially flaked scrapers, both of which are characteristic of Bordes' Quina Mousterian and of the three lowest assemblages at La Quina.

Table 24 gives an indication of reduction intensity on scrapers following Dibble (1988). Convergent, transverse and limace scrapers are grouped and divided by the total number of scrapers for each assemblage. The ratios for the middle-lower beds (7 - M) reflect relatively intensive reduction of scrapers, while the group of uppermost beds (4B-6D) show little to no repeated use of scraper blanks. Although the tool assemblages for the lowest beds (G-L) are dominated by scrapers, it is interesting to note that small numbers of simple serrated edged pieces are also found. An indication of reduction intensity for notched or serrated tools is provided in Table 25. The reduction ratio developed by Dibble (1988) divides denticulates

TABLE 18 - CORE REDUCTION: COUNTS AND PERCENTAGE
(CORES, FLAKES AND TOOLS)

BED	LEVALLOIS	DISC-CORE	N	BED	LEVALLOIS	DISC-CORE
4B	0	19	423	4B	0.00	4.49
6A	0	81	793	6A	0.00	10.21
6A1	1	33	458	6A1	0.22	7.21
6C	0	95	671	6C	0.00	14.16
6D	0	30	958	6D	0.00	3.13
7	1	8	248	7	0.40	3.23
8	14	65	1047	8	1.34	6.21
C	0	2	87	C	0.00	2.30
D	0	6	161	D	0.00	3.73
E	0	6	166	E	0.00	3.61
G	0	6	748	G	0.00	0.80
L	1	5	447	L	0.22	1.12
M	0	1	157	M	0.00	0.64

6364

TABLE 19 - CORES: COUNTS AND PERCENTAGES

BED	DISC	LEVAL	OTHER	N	BED	DISC	LEVAL	OTHER
4B	8	0	1	9	4B	88.89	0.00	11.11
6A	18	0	4	22	6A	81.82	0.00	18.18
6A1	11	0	5	16	6A1	68.75	0.00	31.25
6C	24	0	4	28	6C	85.71	0.00	14.29
6D	9	0	3	12	6D	75.00	0.00	25.00
7	3	1	1	5	7	60.00	20.00	20.00
8	13	0	9	22	8	59.09	0.00	40.91
C	0	0	1	1	C	0.00	0.00	100.00
D	2	0	0	2	D	100.00	0.00	0.00
E	3	0	1	4	E	75.00	0.00	25.00
G	2	0	11	13	G	15.38	0.00	84.62
L	1	0	1	2	L	50.00	0.00	50.00
M	0	0	2	2	M	0.00	0.00	100.00

138

TABLE 20 - KOMBEWA/JANUS FLAKES: COUNTS AND PERCENTAGES

BED	n	%	N
4B	11	2.60	423
6A	24	3.03	793
6A1	10	2.23	448
6C	23	3.43	671
6D	6	0.63	958
7	2	0.81	248
8	10	0.96	1047
C	1	1.15	87
D	3	2.16	139
E	2	1.20	166
G	23	3.07	748
L	15	3.36	447
M	3	1.91	157

TABLE 21 - RETOUCHED FLAKE TOOLS: COUNTS

BED	LIM 8*	STR-SIM 9	CVX-SIM 10	CCV-SIM 11	STR-DBL 12	STR-CVX 13	STR-CVGT 18	CVX-CVGT 19	DEJETE 21	TVSE 22/23	END 30	NOTCH 42/42a	DENT 43	BIF
4B	0	0	0	0	0	0	0	0	0	0	1	15	60	0
6A	0	4	6	0	2	0	1	0	1	0	2	33	66	0
6A1	0	2	0	0	0	0	0	0	0	0	1	16	44	0
6C	0	2	1	0	0	0	0	0	0	0	0	20	66	0
6D	0	8	6	0	2	3	1	0	1	1	0	21	30	8
7	0	1	0	0	0	1	1	0	0	0	0	8	23	0
8	0	5	11	1	0	2	2	5	0	1	2	36	91	0
C	0	0	2	0	0	0	0	0	0	1	0	10	8	0
D	0	0	3	0	0	0	0	0	0	1	0	13	10	0
E	0	2	4	1	0	0	0	0	0	1	1	14	9	0
G	3	9	39	0	0	0	1	5	9	13	0	24	18	0
L	0	9	26	0	0	0	2	5	6	10	2	10	10	0
M	1	2	8	0	0	0	0	0	0	1	0	1	1	0

TABLE 22 - OTHER TOOLS

BED	KNIFE 36-38*	LT RET	IRR RET 45	INT RET 48	ABR RET 49	ALT RET 34	BORER 32	BURIN 3	LEV PT	HMST	SPHERE	N
4B	10	2	4	0	0	0	0	0	0	2	0	18
6A	7	6	10	1	1	1	0	0	0	0	0	26
6A1	6	2	20	0	4	2	0	0	0	0	0	34
6C	15	8	3	3	1	0	0	0	0	0	0	30
6D	6	11	10	0	1	0	0	0	0	0	0	28
7	3	7	4	0	0	0	1	0	0	0	0	15
8	7	14	8	2	0	0	1	1	1	4	1	39
C	1	1	1	0	0	0	0	0	0	0	0	3
D	3	9	2	2	0	0	0	0	0	0	0	16
E	0	3	6	1	1	0	0	0	0	0	0	11
G	1	7	8	0	3	0	0	0	0	1	0	20
L	1	4	5	0	1	0	0	0	0	0	0	11
M	0	0	1	0	0	0	0	0	0	1	0	2

TABLE 23 - MAJOR TOOL GROUPS COUNTS AND PERCENTAGES

BED	NOTCH	DENT	SCR	BIF	OTHER	N	NOTCH	DENT	SCR	BIF	OTHER
4B	15	60	1	0	18	94	15.96	63.83	1.06	0.00	19.15
6A	33	66	16	0	26	141	23.40	46.81	11.35	0.00	18.44
6A1	16	44	3	0	34	97	16.49	45.36	3.09	0.00	35.05
6C	20	66	3	0	30	119	16.81	55.46	2.52	0.00	25.21
6D	21	30	22	8	28	109	19.27	27.52	20.18	7.34	25.69
7	8	23	3	0	15	49	16.33	46.94	6.12	0.00	30.61
8	36	91	29	0	39	195	18.46	46.67	14.87	0.00	20.00
C	10	8	3	0	3	24	41.67	33.33	12.50	0.00	12.50
D	13	10	4	0	16	43	30.23	23.26	9.30	0.00	37.21
E	14	9	9	0	11	43	32.56	20.93	20.93	0.00	25.58
G	24	18	79	0	20	141	17.02	12.77	56.03	0.00	14.18
L	10	10	60	0	11	91	10.99	10.99	65.93	0.00	12.09
M	1	1	12	0	2	16	6.25	6.25	75.00	0.00	12.50

* - Francois Bordes classification number

TABLE 24 - REDUCTION INTENSITY RATIO: SCRAPERS

BED	CVGT, TVSE & LIMACE	TOTAL SCRAPERS	RATIO
4B	0	1	0.00
6A	1	16	0.06
6A1	0	3	0.00
6C	0	3	0.00
6D	2	22	0.09
7	1	3	0.33
8	8	29	0.28
C	1	3	0.33
D	1	4	0.25
E	1	9	0.11
G	22	79	0.28
L	17	60	0.28
M	2	12	0.17

TABLE 25 - REDUCTION INTENSITY RATIO: NOTCHED TOOLS

BED	DENTIC	TOTAL NOTCHED	RATIO
4B	60	75	0.80
6A	66	99	0.67
6A1	44	60	0.73
6C	66	86	0.77
6D	30	51	0.59
7	23	31	0.74
8	91	127	0.72
C	8	18	0.44
D	10	23	0.43
E	9	23	0.39
G	18	42	0.43
L	10	20	0.50
M	1	2	0.50

TABLE 26 - RETOUCH FLAKES: COUNTS AND PERCENTAGES

BED	BIF RET	SCR RET	DENT RET	TOTAL RET	BIF RET	SCR RET	DENT RET
4B	0	22	54	76	0.00	28.95	71.05
6A	2	138	143	283	0.71	48.76	50.53
6A1	13	52	95	160	8.13	32.50	59.38
6C	4	83	152	239	1.67	34.73	63.60
6D	343	264	39	646	53.10	40.87	6.04
7	17	44	30	91	18.68	48.35	32.97
8	9	197	200	406	2.22	48.52	49.26
C	2	25	16	43	4.65	58.14	37.21
D	2	52	19	73	2.74	71.23	26.03
E	0	39	26	65	0.00	60.00	40.00
G	0	257	85	342	0.00	75.15	24.85
L	1	237	26	264	0.38	89.77	9.85
M	1	94	14	109	0.92	86.24	12.84

by the total number of serrated artifacts. Although some notched tools are produced throughout the sequence at La Quina, ratios from Beds 4B - 8 reflect greater reuse of notched tools at the top of the stratigraphic sequence.

The tool collections from Beds C, D and E are small, but they resemble one another. Each bed is characterized by high percentages of denticulates or notches (over 50 per cent in at the top of the stratigraphic sequence.

The tool collections from Beds C, D and E are small, but they resemble one another. Each bed is characterized by high percentages of denticulates or notches (over 50 per cent in each case), medium numbers of scrapers (9-21%) and a few other assorted tool types. Beds C, D and E have too many even edged tools to be considered archetypal Denticulate Mousterian industriess analysis, the assemblages for these upper-middle beds include attributes from both the lower and the upper beds. These strata may represent an intermediate period of change, but they may also be the product of mixing and redeposition.

The tool frequencies for Bed 8 are not typical of any of Bordes' Mousterian groupings, although they can be considered within the realm of a Denticulate Mousterian industry. Bed 8 has a medium proportion (15%) of scrapers and a high proportion (65%) of tools with serrated edges. As Table 25 shows, more than half of these serrated edged tools in Bed 8 were intensively reduced into denticulates. The tools from Bed 8 comprise the largest and most varied assemblage at La Quina, including examples of a limestone sphere, a drill, a burin and a Levallois point (Table 22). Four quartz hammerstones were also recovered from this level.

A number of the upper "midden" beds are dominated by tools with serrated edges. Beds 4B, 6A, 6A1, 6C fit Bordes' (1961) definition of Denticulate Mousterian industries. Each bed is characterized by high numbers of notched and denticulate tools and low percentages of scrapers. These upper beds at La Quina contain 80 per cent (4B), 70 per cent (6A), 62 per cent (6A1), and 72 per cent (6C) tools with notched edges. The lower relative frequency of notched tools in Bed 6A1 may be due to the mixing of artifacts from Bed 7 through Bed 6A in this fill. The extremely high relative frequency of notched artifacts in Bed 4B is complemented by only one scraper and a small number of other artifacts (including two quartz hammerstones) (Table 22). Although the number of tools from Bed 7 is too small to allow definitive interpretation, the percentages of classified artifacts most closely resemble the industry recovered in Beds 8 and 6A (63 per cent denticulate and notched pieces and 6 per cent scrapers).

Bed 6D is distinguished from all of the other beds at La Quina by the presence of bifacial hand axes. Remains of eight small bifaces have been recovered from the sample squares in this stratum. Bed 6D also differs from the other upper beds in having a lower percentage of tools with serrated edges (47%) and a higher percentage of scrapers (20%). The presence of bifaces with a high percentage of denticulates place this assemblage in Bordes' Mousterian of Acheulean Tradition -

Type B (Bordes 1961).

Several generalizations about cultural activity at La Quina can be drawn from these data. First, the frequency of tool types appears to remain constant through several major blocks of geologically defined beds. The tool assemblages of lower and lower-middle strata (G, L and M) do not differ significantly from each other but are significantly different from the upper beds (4B-8). Scrapers predominate in the lower beds, while serrated edged tools are most frequently recovered in the upper beds. Four groupings of beds at La Quina can account for 91 per cent of the variation in relative frequencies of scrapers, denticulates, notched pieces and other tools. A lower group (Beds G-M) is associated by high numbers of scrapers. The second group partitions Bed 6D with Beds C-E. By excluding bifacial tools from this analysis, the assemblage from Bed 6D resembles the even or mixed tool distributions of the middle beds. Beds 4B, 6A1 and 6C are similar to each other in their extremely low frequencies of scrapers (1-3%) and high numbers of denticulate tools. Beds 6A, 7 and 8 have relatively high frequencies of denticulate/notched tools but have more scrapers (6-15%) than Beds 4B, 6A1 and 6C. Tests of association (Kendall's tau) suggest that denticulates, notches and "other" tools all vary together, while scrapers vary separately.

Flakes of Tool Manufacture and Retouch
Where possible, the by-products of tool manufacture and reduction at La Quina were identified in the individually recorded artifact sample. Denticulate retouch, scraper retouch, and biface retouch flakes are used as indicators of specific reduction techniques. "Retouch" flake is used to designate flakes struck from the edge of a tool during manufacture or resharpening. Although this analysis has shown that tool morphology appears to affect assemblage morphology, scraper retouch flakes could be produced during early stages of manufacture of denticulates, bifaces or scrapers. Conversely, Lenoir (1973, 1986) has suggested that notching flakes could be produced in the early stages of scraper reduction, particularly Quina scraper reduction. Table 26 presents the data on retouch flake types as percentages of retouch flakes only. Table 27 shows the frequencies of flakes produced in the production or reduction of certain tool types as a part of the sample of 6392 artifacts.

Scraper retouch flakes show a nearly steady decline in frequency over time. More than half of all retouch flakes in Bed C through Bed M were removed from the edge of a scraper. These data parallel the intensive use of scrapers reflected in the reduction intensity ratio for scrapers in Table 26. In the upper beds, the incidence of scraper retouch flakes generally declines. The frequency of scraper retouch flakes in 6C (35%), 6A1 (33%) and 4B (29%) indicate less production and/or rejuvenation of straight-edged tools during this period. These numbers also parallel the relative frequencies of tools found in these upper beds; Beds 4B, 6A1, and 6C have the lowest percentages of scrapers at La Quina. In contrast, Bed 6A has relatively more scrapers (11%) and more scraper retouch flakes (49%).

Biface retouch and production flakes comprise more than one third (35%) of all individually recorded artifacts and more than 54 per cent of all retouch flakes in Bed 6D. Evidence of bifacial reduction in other beds at La Quina is almost nonexistent. The majority of the other debitage from bifacial reduction occurs in beds contiguous to Bed 6D. Although these flakes may be evidence of bifacial reduction during the deposition of these layers, they are more likely products of movement and mixing. Two-thirds (65%) of the biface retouch flakes in Beds 7 and 8 were recovered in square K1006. The stratigraphic relationship of Beds 6D-8 is distorted and unclear in this section of the site. The elevated frequency of biface retouch flakes in the pit structure (Bed 6A1: 8%) is evidence for post-depositional mixing in this context. Given the extent of the pit, a proportion of flakes from Bed 6D would have been mixed in the fill.

The frequency of denticulate/notch retouch flakes at La Quina gradually increases over time, with the exception of Bed 6D. The least evidence of notch production occurs in Beds M (13%), L (10%) and 6D (6%). Manufacture in each of these beds seems to have been focused on the production of straight-edged tools. The highest percentages of denticulate retouch flakes are found in Beds 6C (64%) and 4B (71%). These beds also contain the highest percentages of notched tools.

Ordered ratios of scraper retouch flakes and denticulate retouch flakes reflect an order similar to that of the partitioning for major tool groups (with the exception of Bed 6D). A relatively low frequency of denticulate retouch flakes in Bed 6D, which may be a statistical artifact of the high frequencies of bifacial retouch flakes in this bed, order this stratum between Beds L and M. Exclusion of bifacial retouch flakes from this analysis also obscures the unique form of reduction found in Bed 6D. With that exception, the data from retouch flakes supports information gained from the analysis of retouched tools. In a general way, these numbers also distinguish the upper from the lower beds. Finally, these data refute the suggestion that any great number of notch retouch flakes were produced in the manufacture of straight edged tools or vice versa.

The total frequency of retouch flakes per bed is an indicator of the relative importance of manufacture and reuse of tools at La Quina. As shown in Table 27, Beds L and M contain many retouch flakes (59% and 69% of all artifacts respectively). Given the low frequencies of cores, chunks, and non-retouch flakes in these beds (Table 1), primary flakes may not have been produced in these contexts at La Quina. With two other exceptions, the frequency of retouch flakes for all other beds is extremely similar. The total number of retouch flakes for these nine beds falls between 49 per cent and 34 per cent with a slight decline in frequency over time. In contrast, two-thirds (65%) of the assemblage of Bed 6D is comprised of retouch flakes, almost all of them produced during the manufacture of straight edged tools (scrapers and bifaces). The production and reduction of bifaces is characterized by quantities of retouch flakes as in Bed 6D at La Quina. At the other end of th*e spectrum, the lowest total percentage of retouch flakes is found in Bed 4B (18%). This assemblage shows little evidence of patterned tool manufacture. There are few cores, chunks, or retouch flakes, but 22 per cent of the assemblage is comprised of tools. The high number of notched tools (80%) and unretouched flakes in Bed 4B may indicate an opportunistic industry with little reuse during this late occupation at La Quina.

Retouch Intensity
An indication of retouch intensity for all flakes and flake tools at La Quina is presented in Table 28. Scars formed during blank manufacture are distinguished from scars formed in marginal flaking after blank production. In this class, artifacts with no evidence of alteration are considered to be unretouched. Artifacts that have been retouched into tools or struck from the edge of a tool are used as indicators of retouch intensity. These numbers suggest extremely intensive use of raw materials at La Quina. With the exception of Bed 4B, more than half of the artifacts recovered at La Quina were made into tools or struck from the edge of a tool. The assemblages from the lowest beds (G, L and M) are dominated by these kinds of flakes (70%, 78%, and 83%). The near absence of flakes without evidence of prior retouch in these beds supports the suggestion that flint arrived at La Quina in a modified form during this period. Using Kendall's tau test, a series of groups of beds (4B; 6A through C & 8 through E; 6D through 7; G, L and M) that account for 94 per cent of total matrix differences are discerned. These groups reflect a general decrease in the intensity of material use over time. The relative frequency of retouched artifacts in Bed 6A1 (62%) is higher than any of the other upper beds and may reflect culling of unretouched artifacts from the pit fill.

METRIC OBSERVATIONS
Flake Size
Length, width, and thickness were measured on complete flakes and on tools in the individually recorded artifact sample. The data are presented in Table 29 through Table 35. The separation of tools and flakes in these analyses helps to reveal variability within and between these two groups. A minimum value, maximum value, median, mean and standard deviation were calculated for each group of artifacts. A "+" sign in the M>M column denotes a median that is greater than the mean of the same population. The difference between the medians for flakes and tools was calculated as was a ratio of flake to tool length.

Table 29 shows that in all cases, the means and medians of flakes selected for use as tool blanks are longer than unretouched flakes. In several cases, the sample median of tools is greater than the mean, denoting a slight negative skew. The greatest differences between tool and flake size are found in the lowest beds (Beds L and M). This evidence again suggests that all stages of reduction are not present in these beds. Large, thick tools appear to have been resharpened and discarded or lost in these contexts. The tools in Bed G are somewhat smaller than in the lowest beds, but the unretouched flakes in G are of similar size to those in L and M. These data support Jelinek's (1988b) suggestion that typologically similar tools were being reduced to different degrees in Beds G, L,

TABLE 27 - RETOUCH FLAKES BY BED:
COUNTS AND PERCENTAGES AS A PART OF ALL ARTIFACTS

BED	BIF RET	SCR RET	DENT RET	TOTAL RET	N	BIF RET	SCR RET	DENT RET	TOTAL RET
4B	0	22	54	76	423	0.00	5.20	12.77	17.97
6A	2	138	143	283	793	0.25	17.40	18.03	35.69
6A1	13	52	95	160	458	2.84	11.35	20.74	34.93
6C	4	83	152	239	671	0.60	12.37	22.65	35.62
6D	343	264	39	646	986	34.79	26.77	3.96	65.52
7	17	44	30	91	248	6.85	17.74	12.10	36.69
8	9	197	200	406	1047	0.86	18.82	19.10	38.78
C	2	25	16	43	87	2.30	28.74	18.39	49.43
D	2	52	19	73	161	1.24	32.30	11.80	45.34
E	0	39	26	65	166	0.00	23.49	15.66	39.16
G	0	257	85	342	748	0.00	34.36	11.36	45.72
L	1	237	26	264	447	0.22	53.02	5.82	59.06
M	1	94	14	109	157	0.64	59.87	8.92	69.43

TABLE 28 - RETOUCH INTENSITY: COUNT AND PERCENTAGES

BED	UNRET	RET	N	UNRET	RET
4B	205	143	348	58.91	41.09
6A	295	375	670	44.03	55.97
6A1	160	269	429	37.30	62.70
6C	263	325	588	44.73	55.27
6D	449	489	938	47.87	52.13
7	108	110	218	49.54	50.46
8	376	576	952	39.50	60.50
C	30	48	78	38.46	61.54
D	60	94	154	38.96	61.04
E	58	100	158	36.71	63.29
G	210	494	704	29.83	70.17
L	94	331	425	22.12	77.88
M	25	121	146	17.12	82.88

TABLE 29 - TOOL AND FLAKE LENGTH

TOOL LENGTH

BED	MIN	MAX	MED	M>M*	MEAN	SD	N
4B	11.29	70.11	40.1	+	38.87	14.54	52
6A	16.90	69.69	31.9		33.67	9.70	61
6A1	8.45	77.66	36.9		37.96	14.50	41
6C	15.28	60.37	35.1	+	34.87	8.95	62
6D	15.53	79.55	37.9		38.03	12.80	40
7	16.57	121.60	33.4		39.92	22.30	26
8	7.25	69.07	37.7	+	36.18	12.08	72
C	8.67	39.15	24.8	+	24.56	11.37	9
D	15.12	43.25	26.8		29.17	8.41	17
E	18.04	77.66	35.3		37.37	14.39	18
G	14.60	77.94	31.4		35.14	14.24	41
L	16.61	75.21	40.4		43.47	16.80	23
M	23.94	70.31	59.5	+	51.26	19.81	3

* "+" denotes a median greater than its mean

FLAKE LENGTH

BED	MIN	MAX	MED	T-F MED	% *	MEAN	SD	N
4B	3.08	85.38	25.5	14.6	64	27.24	14.32	245
6A	4.07	77.80	17.8	14.4	56	20.18	10.90	486
6A1	5.87	88.48	20.0	16.9	54	22.68	13.33	213
6C	4.07	63.10	19.9	15.2	53	21.79	11.15	416
6D	2.00	67.69	17.2	20.7	45	20.82	11.91	395
7	4.19	88.07	20.7	12.7	62	23.60	13.87	116
8	3.60	101.40	16.4	21.3	44	21.81	14.44	603
C	5.76	66.13	15.5	9.3	63	21.90	15.37	42
D	6.62	49.35	15.5	11.3	58	18.28	10.14	85
E	4.40	48.72	20.7	14.6	59	21.45	10.38	77
G	3.07	114.90	20.6	10.8	66	22.03	11.43	422
L	2.90	79.75	17.0	23.4	42	19.68	11.00	269
M	5.35	67.21	15.0	44.5	25	19.26	12.88	113

* median flake length as a % of median tool length

and M.

The difference between the median length of flakes and tools in Bed C is smaller than in the basal strata (Beds G through M). Tool lengths are extremely small, while flake lengths for this bed fall within the general range for La Quina. These numbers suggest that the tools in Bed C were made on smaller flake blanks, perhaps culled from detritus on the slope. Because measurements were taken only on tools for which the original flake size could be discerned, these numbers do not reflect variations in reduction intensity on tools. Measurements on the tools and flakes from Bed D may reflect similar but less intensive use of raw material. The median and average tool and flake lengths decrease between Beds E and C with less difference between the two groups over time.

In the upper beds, tool length remains relatively constant. The tools of Bed 4B appear to be slightly longer than in the other beds, perhaps due to the more casual process of reduction at this time. Flake length is relatively stable throughout this period, although the flakes from Beds 6D and 8 are shorter than the tools in these assemblages. Long, fragile flakes (of bifacial reduction) in these strata may have been subject to and M.

The difference between the median length of flakes and tools in Bed C is smaller than in the basal strata (Beds G through M). Tool lengths are extremely small, while flake lengths for this bed fall within the general range for La Quina. These numbers suggest that the tools in Bed C were made on smaller flake blanks, perhaps culled from detritus on the slope. Because measurements were taken only on tools for which the original flake size could be discerned, these numbers do not reflect variations in reduction intensity on tools. Measurements on the tools and flakes from Bed D may reflect similar but less intensive use of raw material. The median and average tool and flake lengths decrease between Beds E and C with less difference between the two groups over time.

In the upper beds, tool length remains relatively constant. The tools of Bed 4B appear to be slightly longer than in the other beds, perhaps due to the more casual process of reduction at this time. Flake length is relatively stable throughout this period, although the flakes from Beds 6D and 8 are shorter than the tools in these assemblages. Long, fragile flakes (of bifacial reduction) in these strata may have been subject to more breakage.

The data on tool and flake width are presented in Table 30. The range of variation in flake and tool width is much smaller than for length. In both measurements, the difference between flakes and tools is greatest in Beds L and M and slightly reduced in Bed G. With the exception of Beds C and 6D, the difference between median tool width and median flake width is relatively small. Sample size and culling of artifacts in these slope deposits may account for these figures in Bed C. In Bed 6D, the measurements on numbers of relatively narrow bifacial thinning flakes contrast with the measurements of width on proportionately wider tool blanks.

Tool and flake thickness is presented in Table 31. Tool thickness does not vary widely, although the data on tools in Beds C and D again indicate that these artifacts were produced on smaller flakes. The difference between tool and flake thickness is smallest in these two beds and greatest in Beds G - M. These data support the observation that the greatest differences in tool blank size and unretouched flakes occur at the bottom of the La Quina sequence, and the least difference is found in the upper middle beds. The thinnest unretouched flakes are found in Beds 6D, L, and M and the thickest flakes were recovered in Bed 4B. Variation in thickness for flakes in these beds can be explained by differences in manufacture. Bed 6D is dominated by bifacial reduction, while the assemblage of Bed 4B reflects a more opportunistic use of raw material in the production of angular, notched tools. Most of the flakes in Beds L and M were produced during the retouch of scrapers, and these flakes would naturally be thinner than flakes produced during blank production or early stages of lithic reduction.

Width/thickness ratios for tools and flakes are presented in Table 32. The numbers again show that flakes in Bed 6D are relatively thin and flakes in Bed 4B are thicker. The width/thickness ratios for tools are less variable than those for flakes. With the exception of Bed 6D through Bed 8, a decrease over time in mean flake ratios is apparent.

Table 33 through Table 35 present the metric data for spatial distribution in the upper midden beds. Artifacts from the front of the site seem to be the shortest, while objects from squares in the middle and adjacent to the cliff face are generally longer. The flakes and tools on the slope may have been exposed for longer and subject to more reuse and breakage, while objects by the cliff face were covered more quickly and less vulnerable to continued use or damage.

The lithics from the 19 10 x 10 x 5 cm samples were sorted by size. These artifacts were separated in a series of nested screens: 10 mm, 5 mm, 2 mm and .05 mm. The counts and relative frequencies for these data are presented in Table 36. The samples from Beds 6D and 8 contained relatively high numbers of lithics. Small flakes are found in every column sample, but more flakes under 0.5 mm were recovered from Beds 6D and 8 than from Beds 6A and 6C. These data support earlier analyses that showed that lithic reduction in Beds 6A and 6C produced high numbers of unbroken, angular artifacts compared to Beds 6D and 8. Lithics in the samples from Beds G and M are relatively sparse. percentages of various flake sizes fall in between those of the two upper bed groups.

Breakage

Every flake in this La Quina study was classified according to its relative completeness. Table 37 presents the data for individually recorded artifacts, separated into tools and unretouched flakes; Table 38 presents data on completeness from flake bags; and Table 39 presents the data on breakage for the column samples.

The greatest percentage of whole tools is found in Bed 4B

TABLE 30 - TOOL AND FLAKE WIDTH

TOOL WIDTH

BED	MIN	MAX	MED	M>M*	MEAN	SD	N
4B	10.02	49.52	28.9		29.59	8.04	39
6A	13.08	53.15	26.5		27.47	7.53	63
6A1	13.74	48.77	29.0	+	28.60	7.23	29
6C	8.15	52.80	26.5	+	26.35	8.39	56
6D	17.13	46.30	31.5	+	30.77	7.36	49
7	18.00	46.10	27.7		29.69	7.85	25
8	12.03	48.71	28.2		28.78	7.77	79
C	13.03	46.27	30.1	+	28.12	9.05	12
D	13.67	38.96	24.1		24.64	6.05	24
E	14.47	47.68	29.1		31.70	10.33	23
G	24.04	75.08	33.4		36.00	10.48	34
L	14.40	59.33	36.2	+	35.35	10.28	21
M	33.67	37.72	35.7		35.70	2.03	2

* a "+" denotes a median greater than its mean

FLAKE WIDTH

BED	MIN	MAX	T-F MED	MED	MEAN	SD	N
4B	5.45	66.11	23.9	5.0	25.93	10.55	248
6A	2.27	48.09	20.4	6.1	21.06	7.78	486
6A1	8.52	48.71	23.9	5.2	24.22	8.84	181
6C	3.72	49.15	20.5	6.0	21.30	7.97	402
6D	4.55	53.02	18.5	13.0	19.83	8.97	510
7	7.32	84.72	21.6	6.1	23.66	10.94	122
8	5.64	70.86	20.4	7.8	21.61	9.72	639
C	5.94	46.27	18.3	11.8	20.16	9.57	53
D	4.68	40.05	17.2	6.9	17.95	7.16	94
E	6.12	56.77	19.8	9.3	21.80	10.01	75
G	0.83	64.42	20.0	13.4	21.61	21.61	383
L	4.68	58.72	16.5	19.7	19.10	9.86	277
M	5.50	96.10	13.6	22.1	18.00	12.44	115

TABLE 31 - TOOL AND FLAKE THICKNESS

TOOL THICKNESS

BED	MIN	MAX	MED	M>M	MEAN	SD	N
4B	2.77	25.15	8.9		9.07	4.32	62
6A	3.72	18.69	7.8		8.59	3.29	108
6A1	2.43	16.99	8.1		8.25	2.79	41
6C	2.98	17.13	8.5		8.82	3.29	79
6D	2.69	15.46	6.2		6.91	3.03	69
7	3.09	18.70	6.7		7.74	3.63	37
8	1.85	16.37	7.3		7.49	3.08	148
C	2.92	13.20	5.5		6.04	2.48	19
D	2.70	14.91	5.7		6.61	2.85	37
E	2.34	19.03	7.7		8.47	4.19	30
G	3.45	20.31	8.7		9.39	4.20	42
L	3.74	19.37	9.7		10.45	4.21	54
M	2.88	23.00	8.2		10.64	6.74	5

FLAKE THICKNESS

BED	MIN	MAX	MED	T-L MED	MEAN	SD	N
4B	0.61	24.86	6.4	2.5	6.95	4.19	263
6A	0.92	24.81	4.9	2.9	5.71	3.54	555
6A1	0.99	22.33	4.9	3.2	5.53	3.15	212
6C	0.74	16.70	4.9	3.6	5.69	3.29	443
6D	0.58	44.33	2.7	3.5	3.57	3.09	579
7	0.98	13.38	4.4	2.3	4.88	2.71	144
8	0.60	23.10	3.9	3.4	4.93	3.32	690
C	0.77	19.38	3.9	1.6	5.16	3.80	5
D	0.84	14.35	3.8	1.9	4.55	2.71	105
E	0.71	18.64	4.4	3.3	5.46	3.80	97
G	0.42	33.43	4.1	4.6	4.84	3.52	437
L	0.66	28.70	2.9	6.8	4.33	3.71	313
M	0.51	23.56	2.3	5.9	4.00	4.19	127

TABLE 32 - WIDTH/THICKNESS RATIOS: TOOLS AND FLAKES

WIDTH/THICKNESS RATIO: TOOLS

BED	MEAN	SD	VAR	N
4B	4.32	1.63	2.65	39
6A	3.87	1.28	1.63	63
6A1	3.83	0.90	0.82	29
6C	3.35	1.55	2.41	55
6D	5.13	2.06	4.25	49
7	4.56	1.74	3.04	25
8	4.54	2.08	4.34	79
C	4.97	1.84	3.40	12
D	4.11	1.41	1.98	24
E	3.88	1.17	1.37	23
G	4.46	1.48	2.20	34
L	4.50	1.89	3.55	21
M	4.44	0.17	0.03	2

WIDTH/THICKNESS RATIO: FLAKES

BED	MEAN	SD	VAR	N
4B	4.28	2.32	5.36	262
6A	4.48	1.94	3.76	486
6A1	4.83	1.91	3.64	181
6C	4.40	1.86	3.48	401
6D	6.84	2.86	8.20	509
7	5.57	2.31	5.31	122
8	5.34	2.29	5.24	637
C	4.75	1.89	3.59	53
D	4.59	1.89	3.57	93
E	5.01	2.12	4.50	75
G	5.65	2.44	5.93	383
L	5.73	2.03	4.11	277
M	6.21	2.58	6.67	115

TABLE 33 - TOOL AND FLAKE LENGTH BY LOCATION

FRONT: TOOL LENGTH

BED	MIN	MAX	MEAN	SD	N
6A	18.84	47.66	33.22	8.21	11
6C	15.28	60.37	33.48	9.89	26
6D	15.53	52.09	35.49	12.09	15
7	16.57	75.24	37.21	17.99	11
8	8.27	49.55	31.35	11.27	10

FRONT: FLAKE LENGTH

BED	MIN	MAX	MEAN	STD	N
6A	4.76	44.81	16.69	9.42	111
6C	6.24	63.10	21.05	11.05	186
6D	3.35	58.70	17.59	11.25	152
7	6.29	49.08	20.13	11.54	47
8	4.31	57.15	17.65	10.51	155

MIDDLE: TOOL LENGTH

BED	MIN	MAX	MEAN	SD	N
4B	13.62	70.11	39.83	14.38	48
6A	19.31	51.70	33.22	9.45	11
6C	24.40	51.41	39.29	7.41	11
6D	20.87	79.55	39.54	19.01	8
7	18.74	61.96	36.60	14.76	10
8	12.55	65.02	37.17	11.50	36

MIDDLE: FLAKE LENGTH

BED	MIN	MAX	MEAN	STD	N
4B	3.08	74.36	27.23	14.02	224
6A	4.84	55.84	16.97	8.96	71
6C	4.07	58.12	23.64	12.52	70
6D	6.92	60.17	22.87	11.97	58
7	4.19	53.70	25.65	12.81	42
8	4.50	72.84	26.01	14.34	147

BACK: TOOL LENGTH

BED	MIN	MAX	MEAN	SD	N
4B	11.29	42.12	27.38	11.09	4
6A	21.93	69.69	34.37	9.89	38
6C	20.22	50.96	34.37	7.87	25
6D	21.30	58.62	39.56	8.80	17
7	25.42	121.60	52.56	35.22	5
8	7.25	69.07	36.65	12.72	26

BACK: FLAKE LENGTH

BED	MIN	MAX	MEAN	STD	N
4B	8.80	85.38	27.33	17.22	21
6A	4.07	77.80	22.24	11.33	302
6C	5.43	59.43	22.15	10.59	154
6D	2.00	67.69	22.91	11.83	184
7	6.56	88.07	26.44	17.43	27
8	3.60	101.40	21.93	15.62	300

TABLE 34 - TOOL AND FLAKE WIDTH BY LOCATION

FRONT: TOOL WIDTH

BED	MIN	MAX	MEAN	SD	N
6A	17.90	45.84	31.40	8.69	13
6C	8.15	41.44	24.48	7.24	26
6D	18.82	38.58	28.65	6.64	14
7	19.07	46.10	29.83	7.12	10
8	16.09	44.89	28.41	9.64	8

FRONT: FLAKE WIDTH

BED	MIN	MAX	MEAN	SD	N
6A	2.27	40.68	19.05	7.58	115
6C	3.72	49.15	20.14	7.68	174
6D	4.55	48.15	17.67	9.42	137
7	7.32	39.50	19.67	7.18	38
8	5.64	46.49	17.29	8.04	135

MIDDLE: TOOL WIDTH

BED	MIN	MAX	MEAN	SD	N
4B	10.02	49.52	29.69	7.70	33
6A	13.08	33.69	25.25	5.58	11
6C	16.32	39.86	26.24	7.75	13
6D	20.68	46.30	30.81	7.83	10
7	21.47	45.94	29.72	7.78	10
8	14.54	43.22	29.42	6.46	43

MIDDLE: FLAKE WIDTH

BED	MIN	MAX	MEAN	SD	N
4B	5.45	66.11	26.10	10.85	221
6A	6.46	37.26	19.64	6.53	61
6C	7.62	44.15	22.90	8.16	71
6D	7.29	47.27	18.90	8.16	92
7	8.92	49.63	24.10	8.67	43
8	7.74	45.84	23.25	8.41	140

BACK: TOOL WIDTH

BED	MIN	MAX	MEAN	SD	N
4B	16.08	47.85	29.00	9.70	6
6A	3.45	53.15	26.79	7.11	39
6C	14.76	52.80	29.06	9.39	19
6D	17.13	46.07	31.94	7.28	25
7	18.00	45.98	29.36	9.23	5
8	12.03	48.71	27.91	8.86	28

BACK: FLAKE WIDTH

BED	MIN	MAX	MEAN	SD	N
4B	10.88	46.95	24.94	7.37	26
6A	6.02	48.09	22.11	7.89	309
6C	6.37	43.24	22.01	8.13	151
6D	6.03	53.02	21.22	8.76	280
7	8.36	84.72	26.88	14.30	41
8	7.25	65.37	21.77	9.63	343

TABLE 35 - TOOL AND FLAKE THICKNESS BY LOCATION

FRONT: TOOL THICKNESS

BED	MIN	MAX	MEAN	SD	N
6A	4.91	18.69	8.85	3.10	22
6C	3.90	14.90	8.77	3.12	27
6D	2.69	10.44	6.12	2.07	16
7	3.35	18.70	7.59	4.76	11
8	3.27	8.45	6.05	1.80	10

FRONT: FLAKE THICKNESS

BED	MIN	MAX	MEAN	SD	N
6A	1.08	19.12	4.70	3.45	131
6C	0.74	16.50	5.10	2.88	190
6D	0.58	14.49	3.31	2.84	153
7	0.98	10.11	4.02	2.47	48
8	0.60	14.44	3.87	2.71	155

MIDDLE: TOOL THICKNESS

BED	MIN	MAX	MEAN	SD	N
4B	2.77	25.15	9.21	4.48	55
6A	4.02	15.18	9.04	3.21	23
6C	3.29	17.13	9.05	4.04	16
6D	3.01	15.46	8.41	4.27	13
7	3.09	12.78	7.45	2.77	16
8	2.83	16.29	7.66	3.25	71

MIDDLE: FLAKE THICKNESS

BED	MIN	MAX	MEAN	SD	N
4B	0.61	24.86	7.05	4.32	235
6A	1.09	16.10	4.76	2.59	78
6C	1.50	14.31	6.49	3.34	78
6D	0.96	14.06	3.54	2.54	105
7	1.02	13.38	5.32	2.84	50
8	1.02	23.10	5.91	3.72	166

BACK: TOOL THICKNESS

BED	MIN	MAX	MEAN	SD	N
4B	3.71	11.60	7.94	2.43	7
6A	3.72	18.69	8.33	3.36	63
6C	2.98	15.52	8.75	3.01	36
6D	3.44	14.07	6.74	2.68	40
7	3.29	14.05	8.38	3.30	10
8	1.85	16.37	7.52	3.00	67

BACK: FLAKE THICKNESS

BED	MIN	MAX	MEAN	SD	N
4B	1.66	14.69	6.14	2.81	28
6A	0.92	24.81	6.29	3.62	345
6C	1.23	16.70	6.02	3.59	168
6D	0.77	44.33	3.71	3.36	320
7	1.35	10.75	5.32	2.60	46
8	0.89	19.81	4.92	3.23	368

TABLE 36 - COLUMN SAMPLE FLAKE SIZE: COUNTS AND PERCENTAGES

	>10mm	>5mm	>2mm	>.05mm	N	>10mm	>5mm	>2mm	>.05mm
L1005 6A	0	2	6	10	18	0.00	11.11	33.33	55.56
6C	6	26	119	68	219	2.74	11.87	54.34	31.05
6D	2	12	155	155	324	0.62	3.70	47.84	47.84
8	12	36	154	66	268	4.48	13.43	57.46	24.63
M1005 6A	5	10	33	5	53	9.43	18.87	62.26	9.43
	4	10	25	13	52	7.69	19.23	48.08	25.00
6C	4	15	42	*	61	6.56	24.59	68.85	*
	15	28	33	*	76	19.74	36.84	43.42	*
6D	5	8	73	61	147	3.40	5.44	49.66	41.50
	3	22	83	58	166	1.81	13.25	50.00	34.94
8	7	23	147	46	223	3.14	10.31	65.92	20.63
	22	42	222	93	379	5.80	11.08	58.58	24.54
N1004 6A	5	6	13	4	28	17.86	21.43	46.43	14.29
6C	6	5	20	5	36	16.67	13.89	55.56	13.89
6D	8	20	90	63	181	4.42	11.05	49.72	34.81
H1005 G	6	13	43	3	65	9.23	20.00	66.15	4.62
	10	13	50	2	75	13.33	17.33	66.67	2.67
F1006 M	3	5	11	3	22	13.64	22.73	50.00	13.64
	1	0	11	3	15	6.67	0.00	73.33	20.00

* sediment unavailable for analysis

(72%) and the lowest percentage in Bed 6D (34%). These data, which parallel analyses of other variables at La Quina, can be explained by technological factors. The high incidence of breakage in Bed 6D is probably tied to the manufacture of bifaces and the production of extremely thin, fragile flakes and flake tools. The low incidence of breakage in Bed 4B is related to the quantity of thick, angular tools found in this context. It is interesting to note that the frequency of broken tools is higher in the pit structure (6A1: 54%), as it is suspected that this material was removed and replaced several times. Relative frequencies for broken tools from the remaining beds at La Quina fall between 50 per cent and 35 per cent.

The frequency of whole and broken unretouched flakes also vary significantly by bed. The data on flakes and tools are similar, although more flakes than tools are whole. Many more flakes than tools were produced, and tools were less likely to have been discarded if not broken. With the exception of Bed 6D, whole flakes comprise more than half of the artifacts recorded for each bed. The highest numbers of whole flakes are found in Beds 4B (81%), 6A (76%), 6C (80%), C (75%), L (74%) and M (76%). In contrast to all of the other beds, broken flakes dominate the assemblage of Bed 6D (56%). Almost half of the flakes in Bed 6A1 (43%) were broken.

Split tools and flakes appear to occur in a random fashion. This class of objects does not vary consistently with whole or broken flakes. Although there are generally more split flakes than split tools, no patterns of variation between the two artifact classes was found.

Table 38 presents the data on breakage of flakes from excavation and screen bags. Not surprisingly, the numbers of broken flakes in these bags are much higher than for individual artifacts. The patterns of variation between beds remain similar. The highest percentages of whole flakes are found at the top of the site (Bed 4B: 41%), and the lowest proportion of whole flakes is found in Bed 6D (9%).

The incidence of shatter does not vary greatly between beds, although Bed 4B contains a high frequency of these irregular lithic pieces and Bed 6D has a low frequency (2%). These numbers support the interpretation of lithic angularity in Bed 4B and regularity and fragility in Bed 6D. Shatter from flake bags can be considered analogous to chunks in the individually recorded sample. The data on chunks in Table 1 parallel the information on shatter in Table 38.

Data on flake breakage for the 19 column samples are presented in Table 39. In a very broad way, these data also parallel the information from the individual and flake bag analysis. The samples from Beds 6A, G, and M have more whole flakes, while the samples from Bed 6D have the least. As in the flake bag sample, these artifacts have a relatively high tendency to be broken compared to the large artifacts.

Table 40 presents the data for completeness for individually recorded artifacts in the front, middle and back of the upper beds. The frequencies suggest that objects toward the front of the site have the greatest tendency to be broken. Artifacts in the middle units show the least tendency for breakage.

Assemblages with evidence of core reduction had greater numbers of whole flakes, but high relative frequencies of whole flakes were also found in assemblages with evidence of opportunistic tool manufacture (Bed 4B) and assemblages of tool rejuvenation (Beds L and M). Broken flakes are more closely associated with tool manufacture than with core reduction, as a high incidence of flake breakage associated with bifacial tool manufacture in Bed 6D demonstrates. In the upper beds, shatter appears associated with core reduction rather than tool rejuvenation or manufacture.

Weight
Bone, limestone, lithics, and soil from the column samples were weighed by material. The numbers on Table 41 reflect the extremely high anthropogenic component of the site. The highest quantities of cultural material are found in Beds 8 and 6C, suggesting that the most intensive site use occurred at this time. The finest sediment from the upper "midden" levels still contains quantities of tiny burned bone fragments that would further contribute to the cultural component of these beds. In the lower strata, none of the bone is burned and no fragments of bone are included in the sandy soil. These strata (Beds G and M) have fairly high proportions of bone, but generally less lithic material. The lesser amount of cultural material is particularly evident in Bed M. In contrast, the relative weight of limestone fragments (*éboulis*) in Bed M is extremely high.

Burned Flakes
Table 42 gives the frequencies for burned flakes recovered from excavation and screen flake bags. The percentages of burned flakes are relatively low for all beds at La Quina, but frequencies are higher in the upper beds. These data correspond with the increased incidence of burned bone in the upper "midden" layers. A relatively high frequency of burned flakes in the upper-middle beds (D and E) is also apparent and may result from redepostion of the midden deposits on the slope.

Conclusion
In almost every category of this analysis a gradual or marked change between the upper and lower beds was discerned. While the retouched tools of the lower beds are primarily scrapers, the edges on the retouched tools from the upper beds are predominantly notched or denticulated. Analysis of the non-retouched tool component of the La Quina assemblages revealed that only evidence of late-stage manufacture is found in the lower beds with the scrapers. A more complete and varied representation of lithic reduction is found in the upper beds. Analysis of the full lithic component from the upper beds indicate that core reduction and tool manufacture occurred here. These analyses of the La Quina lithic assemblages suggest that raw material was being used differentially in the upper and lower beds. Non-lithic data (i.e. faunal, geologic and floral analyses) will be integrated with the lithic information for each assemblage. The variation recognized at La Quina can then be related to Middle

TABLE 37 - BREAKAGE: COUNTS AND PERCENTAGES

TOOLS

BED	WHOLE	BROKEN	SPLIT	N	BED	WHOLE	BROKEN	SPLIT
4B	66	22	4	92	4B	71.74	23.91	4.35
6A	81	56	4	141	6A	57.45	39.72	2.84
6A1	45	52	0	97	6A1	46.39	53.61	0.00
6C	72	44	2	118	6C	61.02	37.29	1.69
6D	37	70	2	109	6D	33.94	64.22	1.83
7	30	17	2	49	7	61.22	34.69	4.08
8	106	85	3	194	8	54.64	43.81	1.55
C	12	10	1	23	C	52.17	43.48	4.35
D	23	19	1	43	D	53.49	44.19	2.33
E	22	20	1	43	E	51.16	46.51	2.33
G	74	66	0	140	G	52.86	47.14	0.00
L	54	36	1	91	L	59.34	39.56	1.10
M	8	8	0	16	M	50.00	50.00	0.00

FLAKES

BED	WHOLE	BROKEN	SPLIT	N	BED	WHOLE	BROKEN	SPLIT
4B	233	47	7	287	4B	81.18	16.38	2.44
6A	438	106	34	578	6A	75.78	18.34	5.88
6A1	172	139	10	321	6A1	53.58	43.30	3.12
6C	382	80	18	480	6C	79.58	16.67	3.75
6D	349	474	18	841	6D	41.50	56.36	2.14
7	93	73	8	174	7	53.45	41.95	4.60
8	556	192	23	771	8	72.11	24.90	2.98
C	43	13	1	57	C	75.44	22.81	1.75
D	77	30	5	112	D	68.75	26.79	4.46
E	64	46	6	116	E	55.17	39.66	5.17
G	365	183	29	577	G	63.26	31.72	5.03
L	250	68	22	340	L	73.53	20.00	6.47
M	100	28	4	132	M	75.76	21.21	3.03

TABLE 38 - BREAKAGE: FLAKE BAGS (COUNTS AND PERCENTAGES)

BED	WHL	BRKN	SHTR	N	BED	WHL	BRKN	SHTR
4B	215	262	42	519	4B	41.43	50.48	8.09
6A	492	995	65	1552	6A	31.70	64.11	4.19
6A1	140	414	17	571	6A1	24.52	72.50	2.98
6C	299	518	41	858	6C	34.85	60.37	4.78
6D	224	2383	51	2658	6D	8.43	89.65	1.92
7	148	497	23	668	7	22.16	74.40	3.44
8	403	1111	83	1597	8	25.23	69.57	5.20
C	124	255	18	397	C	31.23	64.23	4.53
D	209	774	16	999	D	20.92	77.48	1.60
E	90	225	20	335	E	26.87	67.16	5.97
G	186	595	23	804	G	23.13	74.00	2.86
L	134	325	21	480	L	27.92	67.71	4.38
M	50	122	10	182	M	27.47	67.03	5.49

TABLE 39 - BREAKAGE: COLUMN SAMPLES - COUNTS AND PERCENTAGES

	WHL	BRKN	SHTR	N		WHL	BRKN	SHTR
L1005 6A	2	16	0	18		11.11	88.89	0.00
6C	22	181	16	219		10.05	82.65	7.31
6D	5	312	7	324		1.54	96.30	2.16
8	21	226	21	268		7.84	84.33	7.84
M1005 6A	10	38	5	53		18.87	71.70	9.43
	10	38	4	52		19.23	73.08	7.69
6C	4	57	0	61		6.56	93.44	0.00
	9	62	5	76		11.84	81.58	6.58
6D	12	133	2	147		8.16	90.48	1.36
	5	157	4	166		3.01	94.58	2.41
8	12	206	5	223		5.38	92.38	2.24
	39	333	7	379		10.29	87.86	1.85
N1004 6A	7	21	0	28		25.00	75.00	0.00
6C	5	30	1	36		13.89	83.33	2.78
6D	9	171	1	181		4.97	94.48	0.55
H1005 G	24	41	0	65		36.92	63.08	0.00
	27	45	3	75		36.00	60.00	4.00
F1006 M	7	15	0	22		31.82	68.18	0.00
	3	11	1	15		20.00	73.33	6.67

TABLE 40 - BREAKAGE BY LOCATION: COUNTS AND PERCENTAGES

	FRONT				MIDDLE				BACK		
BED	WHOLE	BRKN	N		WHOLE	BRKN	N		WHOLE	BRKN	N
4B					281	91	372		32	10	42
6A	126	41	167		85	29	114		350	139	489
6C	218	63	281		83	22	105		183	67	250
6D	143	279	422		75	57	132		188	231	419
7	45	51	96		59	28	87		36	24	60
8	126	141	267		199	66	265		361	131	492
N	658	575	1233		782	293	1075		1150	602	1752

	FRONT			MIDDLE			BACK	
BED	WHOLE	BRKN		WHOLE	BRKN		WHOLE	BRKN
4B				75.54	24.46		76.19	23.81
6A	75.45	24.55		74.56	25.44		71.57	28.43
6C	77.58	22.42		79.05	20.95		73.20	26.80
6D	33.89	66.11		56.82	43.18		44.87	55.13
7	46.88	53.13		67.82	32.18		60.00	40.00
8	47.19	52.81		75.09	24.91		73.37	26.63
N	53.37	46.63		72.74	27.26		65.89	34.11

TABLE 41 - MATERIAL BY WEIGHT IN GRAMS: COLUMN SAMPLES

		BONE	LIMEST	LITHICS	SOIL	TOTAL
L1005	6A	13.5	93.5		49.0	156.0
	6C	112.5	366.5	24.5	228.0	731.5
	6D	38.5	275.0	8.5	204.0	526.0
	8	175.5	251.5	26.0	228.0	681.0
M1005	6A	157.0	390.5	9.0	210.0	766.5
		64.5	312.5	5.0	143.5	525.5
	6C	112.5	258.0	10.5	*	381.0
		122.0	382.0	35.5	*	539.5
	6D	50.0	483.0	9.0	197.0	739.0
		97.5	197.5	8.0	172.5	475.5
	8	114.5	152.0	15.5	15.5	297.5
		172.5	300.0	49.5	315.0	837.0
N1004	6A	40.5	380.5	6.5	111.0	538.5
	6C	106.5	164.0	8.0	127.0	405.5
	6D	44.5	181.0	13.5	131.5	370.5
H1005	G	155.0	391.0	5.5	52.0	603.5
		180.0	405.0	12.5	75.0	672.5
G1006	M	135.0	745.0	6.0	140.0	1026.0
		37.0	715.0	2.5	106.0	860.5

		BONE	LIMEST	LITHICS	SOIL	
L1005	6A	8.65	59.94	0.00	31.41	
	6C	15.38	50.10	3.35	31.17	
	6D	7.32	52.28	1.62	38.78	
	8	25.77	36.93	3.82	33.48	
M1005	6A	20.48	50.95	1.17	27.40	
		12.27	59.47	0.95	27.31	
	6C	29.53	67.72	2.76	*	
		22.61	70.81	6.58	*	
	6D	6.77	65.36	1.22	26.66	
		20.50	41.54	1.68	36.28	
	8	38.49	51.09	5.21	5.21	
		20.61	35.84	5.91	37.63	
N1004	6A	7.52	70.66	1.21	20.61	
	6C	26.26	40.44	1.97	31.32	
	6D	12.01	48.85	3.64	35.49	
H1005	G	25.68	64.79	0.91	8.62	
		26.77	60.22	1.86	11.15	
F1006	M	13.16	72.61	0.58	13.65	
		4.30	83.09	0.29	12.32	*trace

TABLE 42 - BURNED FLAKES FROM FLAKE BAGS: COUNTS AND PERCENTAGES

BED	n	f	N
4B	0	0.00	519
6A	8	0.52	1552
6A1	1	0.18	571
6C	19	2.21	858
6D	3	0.11	2658
7	7	1.05	668
8	58	3.63	1597
C	0	0.00	397
D	24	2.40	999
E	3	0.91	329
G	0	0.00	804
L	0	0.00	480
M	0	0.00	182

Paleolithic economy and settlement.

57

CHAPTER VI

INTERPRETATION OF LITHIC VARIABILITY

Introduction

This chapter presents the interpretation of the variation in lithic attributes revealed through analyses in Chapter V. Many of the attributes investigated in this analysis vary together. Much of this variation is related to restrictions imposed by the mechanical properties of lithic reduction. The amount of cortex, the shape, the thickness, and the external scar morphology of a flake and its platform are all interrelated and reflect variation in stages and technique of reduction. For example, flakes produced in the reduction of a biface are thin, have little cortex, many exterior scars, and faceted platforms. In contrast, products from early stages of lithic reduction tend to be thicker with more cortex and fewer scars on their exterior or platform. Changes in the intensity and technology of lithic reduction will be examined and interpreted in this chapter. Variations in artifact class, raw material, reduction technique, artifact size, and completeness also reflect differences in economy and subsistence. Implications from this lithic analysis are combined with faunal and other environmental data where possible.

Analysis by Stratum

At the base of the La Quina sequence is a group of beds (G, L and M) whose tool assemblages are dominated by scrapers. These beds also have extremely high frequencies (half of all classified artifacts) of flakes struck from the edge of a tool (i.e. biface, scraper, or denticulate retouch flakes). The majority of these artifacts have been identified as products of scraper manufacture or rejuvenation. The near absence of cores and the limited numbers of angular flakes, chunks, or shatter suggest that little or no primary reduction occurred at La Quina during this time. Instead of nodule reduction or flake production, lithic activity appears to have focused on resharpening tools that had been at least roughly shaped elsewhere. Low numbers of flakes with cortex support this interpretation. These beds also contain relatively less cultural material than the other beds at La Quina, especially in terms of lithic artifacts, as reflected in the two column samples from Bed M.

The fauna in each of the beds at La Quina is mostly reindeer, equid, and bovid. In Beds L and M, the bones of bovids are most prevalent and occur in large fragments. All parts of the skeleton appear to be represented. Given the numbers of broken and disarticulated animal bone in these layers it is likely that butchering game was the primary activity practiced at La Quina at this time. Geological evidence suggests that the Voultron River was at a high level, although water action was not vigorous. Ponds and marshes at the margins of the valley would have afforded good areas to mire animals that had been frightened over the cliff or along the valley floor, but not good places to manufacture tools. No pollen from these layers has yet been identified.

The interpretation of butchering activity in the lower beds is also supported by the presence of quartz cobble hammerstones and shaped bone percussion tools. Whether these objects were used to rejuvenate lithics or to smash bones, they represent a relatively opportunistic acquisition of raw materials. The few cores found in these lowest beds are larger and less prepared than those in the upper beds. These artifacts may, like the quartz cobbles, represent local resource acquisition. Nearly all of the other lithic material in these assemblages is in a previously reduced state.

Relatively high numbers of complete flakes in the two lowest beds may also indicate limited lithic manufacturing, although it may also be the result of accumulation of lithic objects under boggy conditions. In Beds L and M the relative frequency of complete flakes is over 70 per cent.

Butchering and tool rejuvenation appear to have been the primary activities at La Quina throughout the deposition of Bed G, but this deposition occurred under drier and colder conditions. The faunal assemblage contains fewer and smaller bone fragments than the lowest beds and greater quantities of *éboulis*. The faunal assemblage from Bed G is predominantly comprised of reindeer bones, indicating conditions of intense cold.

The relative frequency of complete flakes in Bed G is 63 per cent. If the sediments of Bed G reflect drier conditions, these lithics could have been exposed longer and been more easily damaged or reused. Differences in size between flakes and tools tend to confirm this suggestion. In Beds L and M, tools are larger and flakes are smaller than in Bed G. In Bed G, tools may not have been as quickly lost, allowing more breakage and more reuse. None of the heavily reduced tools were measured in this analysis, so the metric data can only indicate tool blank size. Measurements on the heavily retouched tool component of this assemblage would be necessary to demonstrate that tools were more heavily reduced in Bed G than in the basal strata. However, the median and mean for Bed G tool lengths suggest that smaller tool blanks were being recovered and used in this context.

More than half of the tools in these three lower beds are scrapers and more than half of the remaining lithic artifacts are scraper retouch flakes. Artifact class frequencies for Bed G are more evenly distributed than in Beds L and M. These numbers suggest that a slightly wider range of reduction techniques was employed during the deposition of the early middle strata at La Quina. Bed G was excavated in three sub-layers: G1, G2, and G3. In order to increase the sample size, the lithics from these three sub-levels were combined for the purposes of this study. An analysis of the Bed G lithic assemblages by Jelinek (n.d.) showed that the uppermost of these three beds, G1, had a predominance of notched and denticulate tools, while the tool assemblages of lower levels, Beds G2 and G3, are dominated by heavily reduced scrapers. His analysis suggests a transition in tool morphology at this point.

Although the sample collections from Beds C, D and E are extremely small, several observations can be made. First, these three beds have the highest relative frequencies of tools at La Quina. Tools represent more than a quarter of each assemblage. Second, the tool types of these middle beds are more varied than in the lower beds. The relative increase in notched or denticulate tools is particularly notable. The assemblages from Beds C, D and E are dominated by products of tool production and reduction. The low number of cores and technological by-products of core preparation/reduction in the upper-middle beds suggests that this activity was not common, although perhaps more so than at the base of the sequence. The focus on tool reduction is similar to that in the lower beds, but a broader distribution of retouch flake forms in Beds C, D and E reflects the broader range of tool forms that were being produced and reduced. The higher percentages of multi-faceted platforms in these beds also reflect variation in technology and a greater segment of the reduction sequence. Elevated frequencies of broken flakes in the upper-middle beds may be related to a greater emphasis on tool manufacture or to natural forces of deposition. Finally, the tools in Beds C through E are not substantially larger than the unretouched flakes. These data suggest that smaller blanks were being utilized in this context. Evidence for the re-deposition of these upper-middle strata may have contributed to this size distribution; larger tools or tool blanks may have been periodically removed from the exposed material. The intensive use of raw material may also account for the high frequencies of tools in these beds. A number of these attributes suggest that at least Bed C represents material that was pushed off and moved down slope from the horizontal platform at the top of the massive colluvium that underlies the base of the "midden" beds.

The sample from Bed 8 at the base of these "midden" deposits is the largest in the La Quina sample. Not surprisingly, its content is also the most varied as diversity increases with sample size. Recent studies (Jones *et al.* 1989, Thomas 1989) have shown that such diversity in tool class is also associated with more intensive site use. Evidence of more varied techniques of core and tool production are found in Bed 8 than in any other bed. Although greater numbers of notched tools are found than scrapers, the retouch flakes reflect equal emphasis on the production of straight and serrated edges. Reduction ratios for these major tools groups suggest that the reduction of notched tools was more intensive in this context than in the lower beds; scrapers were less intensively utilized than below. The tool assemblage of Bed 8 also includes examples of tools such as a burin, Levallois point, and limestone spheres, not found in other beds at La Quina. Examples of both Levallois and disc-core reduction are also present. Relatively high levels of cortex on flakes and multi-faceted platforms suggest that debitage from a variety of manufacturing stages is also represented in Bed 8. These lines of evidence indicate that a wider range of activities were conducted during this period than earlier or later in time.

The sediments of Bed 8 include the highest anthropogenic content of all the beds at La Quina. Much of the cultural material is burned and unburned reindeer bone. This predominance of reindeer bone indicates that this was a period of relatively intense cold. Bed 8 is also the oldest bed to show evidence of the use of fire in its lithic and faunal assemblages. Bed 8 data suggest the first domestic activity at La Quina. Given the limited amounts of *éboulis* and the short time frame allotted by absolute dates for the accumulation of all of the upper beds, the high anthropogenic content of Bed 8 indicates that this domestic activity was relatively intensive.

The remaining "midden" beds also reflect periods of greater domestic activity than the lower beds. Although a greater emphasis on notched and denticulate tools is found in the upper levels, a variety of tool forms are present. Indications of core reduction such as cores, chunks, disc-core flakes are generally more prevalent in the upper beds than the lower ones and the frequencies of tools are proportionately lower. With the exception of Bed 6D, the percentages of retouch flakes are lower overall and reflect more diversity in the upper beds than the lower or middle beds. Bed 6D is the only upper bed to show lower frequencies of cortical flakes than the basal strata. High relative frequencies of flakes with cortex in the other upper beds suggest that more complete sequences of reduction are represented in these contexts. Although many similarities exist between the assemblages from the upper beds, differences among them exist.

The sample from Bed 7 is smaller than that from Bed 8, but it is roughly similar in composition. This comparability may be due to the fact that Bed 7 represents an attenuation of Bed 8 activities. Variation in the frequencies of artifact classes between Beds 7 and 8 can be explained by some post-depositional mixing of Bed 7 with Bed 6D. Geological indications of extreme cold in Bed 7 indicate that La Quina may not have been occupied during the deposition and decomposition of some of the sediments that comprise this stratum. In that case, the cultural material in the Bed 7 assemblage may have been displaced from strata deposited previously and subsequently.

Evidence from faunal and floral analysis suggest that all of the Bed 6 strata were deposited under conditions of less intense cold than during the deposition of Bed 7. The bones from these beds represent a mixture of bovids and equids with lower frequencies of reindeer, while the pollen suggests an increase in local arboreal elements. Analysis of the microvertebrates from these strata may someday more precisely indicate the nature of this environment. For now, climatological distinctions between the Bed 6 strata cannot be made.

Bed 6D is technologically and typologically distinct from all of the other beds at La Quina. As in Bed 8, the tool assemblage from Bed 6D is relatively varied, but there is a greater emphasis on straight edged tools than in the other upper strata. In partitioned G-Square, the Bed 6D retouched tools were associated with Beds C through E when bifaces were excluded from analysis. Bifacial reduction flakes dominate the Bed 6D assemblage. The total percentage of retouch flakes (65%) is only surpassed in Bed M. Related to the high numbers of biface retouch flakes are low percentages of flakes with exterior cortex, low numbers of flakes with cortical or plain platforms, low average flake thickness, and more broken lithics. The quantities of (bifacial) retouch flakes make this industry appear similar in several of the analyses to the scraper-rich assemblages of the lower strata that have numerous (scraper) retouch flakes. Although an emphasis on the production and reduction of bifaces in Bed 6D is evident, the rest of the 6D lithic assemblage does not dramatically differ from the other upper "midden" beds.

The assemblage from Bed 6C offers the best evidence at La Quina for a full sequence of lithic reduction on cores and notched tools. First, the frequencies of cores and chunks (many of which resemble heavily reduced cores) are relatively high in this bed. A high percentage of these cores and flakes are products of disc-core reduction. High frequencies of flakes with exterior cortex and simple platforms were also found. These attributes suggest that debitage from early stages of nodule reduction and flake manufacture is present in this assemblage. Bed 6C is also notable for its high percentage of burned flakes and its relatively high density of cultural material.

The assemblage from Bed 6A resembles Bed 6C in its emphasis on the manufacture of notched edged tools and radial core reduction. The assemblage differs in its slightly lower frequencies of notched tools and higher numbers of scrapers. The relative frequencies of retouch flakes parallel these differences. Bed 6A also has a slightly lower relative frequency of cortical flakes and a higher percentage of large whole flakes than Bed 6C.

The assemblage from Bed 6A1 (the pit feature) appears to be a mixture of material from Beds 6D through 6A. This mixing of several assemblages has had the effect of neutralizing any variation that existed between the beds. In almost all lithic classes, the material in Bed 6A1 shows frequencies close to but more evenly distributed than those of Beds 6C and 6A. The recovery of several biface retouch flakes in Bed 6A1 suggests the inclusion of fill that originated in Bed 6D. The excavated form of the pit, which reaches the top of Bed 8, supports this interpretation. The assemblage from Bed 6A1 has a higher frequency of tools than the surrounding beds. The frequency of retouched artifacts in Bed 6A1 suggests that usable, unretouched flakes were being culled during excavation, re-excavation, or backfill of the structure. High relative frequencies of broken objects in this bed may also support this interpretation. In contrast, the size of tools and flakes in Bed 6A1 is as great as, or greater than, those in the surrounding strata. The material within the pit appears to have been mixed and redeposited at least once, but the purpose of this activity is still unclear. The hypothesis of meat storage in this feature is plausible, but perhaps impossible to prove. Soil samples from the bottom of the pit have been saved for eventual analysis.

The collection from Bed 4B reflects an industry dominated by the production of notched tools. High percentages of cortical flakes, cortical platforms, and unretouched objects indicate that early-stage lithic reduction was carried out, and that reuse was much less intensive than during other cultural episodes. The metric data for this bed show that only relatively large flakes were transformed into tools. The focus on notch/denticulate production gives the assemblage a blocky, angular character with high relative flake thickness. High frequencies of whole flakes are probably the result of this reduction pattern. Although the same species of animals are represented in the assemblage from this bed as in the other upper beds, these bones have been treated differently. The bone fragments have not been pulverized or burned, but are large and often articulated. Hammerstones in this context may have been used to obtain marrow, as in the lower beds. Evidence from this assemblage suggests a focus on hunting and butchering. In contrast to the assemblages associated with short-term butchering activity in the lower beds, these lithics are not heavily reduced. The recovered objects, most of them denticulates, appear to have been made from locally available material to meet immediate needs. Although the predominant tool form is different in the earliest and latest La Quina strata, similarities between these assemblages suggest that both represent a small number of butchering episodes. Differences in the edge morphology of tools in the lowest and the last beds do not appear to correlate with functional differences associated with subsistence activity, but may be related to differences in habitat. In Beds L and M artifacts may have been lost rather than reused; in Bed 4B the available usable space at La Quina may have become restricted, precluding reoccupation.

Cultural Patterns
In the La Quina assemblages, variation has been recognized between beds, between groups of beds, and within the site as a whole. The preceding discussion focused on variation between individual beds or sets of beds. Changes in tool form and intensity of reduction at La Quina have been correlated with environmental data from the site. The relationship of these broad patterns of variation to changes in land use patterns will be explored next.

A primary aspect of lithic variation at La Quina is observed in the edge morphology of tools. A dichotomy between even and serrated edged tools has been recognized by Rolland (1977, 1981, 1988a) and Barton (1988, 1989) in their studies of French and Iberian Middle Paleolithic assemblages. At La Quina, the reduction of scrapers dominates in the lower layers while production of denticulate tools dominates in the upper beds. With the exclusion of Bed 6D, the emphasis on straight edged tools declines over time. Almost every analysis of lithic variability introduced in the previous chapter found broad differences between the upper and lower sets of beds. These differences were less distinct in the middle layers of the site. Bed 6D was occasionally associated with the lower beds through its predominance of (bifacial) retouch flakes and number of scrapers.

Debitage from different stages and types of reduction has been distinguished through this analysis. The production and reduction of different edge types results in debitage with different traits. An emphasis on the production of notched-edged pieces results in an industry with a number of blocky, angular lithic artifacts. The reduction of scrapers leaves flakes that are neither angular nor flat but thin, and with a rounded or a short/wide form. Bifacial reduction can be detected by quantities of long, flat non-cortical flakes with heavily faceted platforms. The analysis of the unretouched lithic artifacts from the La Quina assemblages suggests that certain types of lithic activity are associated with each tool edge type. Intensive scraper reduction in the lower beds is not associated with core reduction or the intensive manufacture and reduction of notched tools. Notched pieces are more likely to be recovered with artifacts from core reduction and early stage tool manufacture than with scrapers, as illustrated in the upper beds.

The tool and faunal evidence indicate that the industries in the lower beds at La Quina are the result of short-term activities centered on the butchering of game. Pre-shaped tools that could be quickly and easily resharpened were brought to the site. The lithic assemblages from the lower beds at La Quina are dominated by in heavily reduced scrapers and scraper retouch flakes. There is little indication of any early-stage lithic reduction. A number of simple, notched tools were imported or produced during this period, but the relative frequency of denticulates is low in these beds. Much later in time, La Quina appears to have used more intensively. A greater variety in lithic technology and stages of lithic manufacture are found in the upper beds. Straight edged tools were produced and rejuvenated, but the focus of tool reduction was on serrated edged tools. The emphasis on heavily utilized notched tools increased over time. These "midden" deposits are largely composed of fragmented and burned bone with little non-cultural material. The quantities of bone in the upper layers suggest that hunting was an important subsistence activity, but it has not been demonstrated whether primary butchering was carried out elsewhere or whether notched tools were being used for these purposes. Association of notched tools with large and sometimes articulated bone fragments in Bed 4B may indicate that serrated tools were used for butchering in this context.

Conclusion

As discussed in Chapter II, the interrelationship of mobility and the acquisition and use of raw material appears to vary in response to local climate and resources. The models proposed by Barton (1989), Munday (1976), and Rolland and Dibble (1990) suggest that lithic reduction sequences must be considered in light of environmental factors. Geological and faunal evidence indicate that the lower, middle, and early upper beds at La Quina were deposited under conditions of increasing cold. The analysis of the lithic assemblages showed that site use was sporadic and of short duration until the deposition of Bed 8. Most of the tools from the lower and middle beds were imported in a reduced form, although quartz cobbles and local flint were also used. In contrast, the Bed 8 assemblage represents more intensive long-term occupation under continued cold conditions. The lithics are more varied in morphology and technology. Following a period of abandonment (Bed 7), the temperature began to rise. Occupation of the site was again relatively intensive throughout the deposition of Bed 6 and there is an increased emphasis on angular notched pieces in these assemblages. Tool production was more opportunistic and disc-core reduction more prevalent in these upper beds. The latest cultural remains examined from La Quina (Bed 4B) indicate short-term activity with casual

early-stage manufacture.

Some of the variation in lithic manufacture and reduction recognized at La Quina may be related to patterns of mobility recognized elsewhere. As Kelly (1985, 1988) has suggested, mobile peoples often carry pre-formed tools or cores. Bifaces can be used in this manner, but so can other tool forms such as scrapers. During periods of greater sedentism, access to raw material is assured and tools tend to be more opportunistically or expediently prepared. At La Quina, the basal assemblages reflect task-specific site use during periods of moderate to extreme cold. The tools in these assemblages, largely scrapers, were apparently prepared at another location and carried to La Quina. Evidence of more tool manufacture and core preparation in the upper beds suggest that the site was used for longer periods of time with a more varied range of activities. Scrapers were not being manufacture or reduced in large numbers. This evidence for increased sedentism correlates with a rise in temperature.

Although data from other sites are needed, analyses of raw materials by Geneste (1985, 1989), Meignen (1988), Roebroeks *et al.* (1988) and Jelinek (1991) reflect similar patterns of raw material exploitation at other Middle Paleolithic sites. Material closest at hand tends to be the most abundant in a site and the least intensely reduced. In contrast, material gathered from longer distances occurs in lower frequencies and is more subject to patterned reduction. Dibble, Roth, and Lenoir (1995) and Kuhn (1992) caution that direct intent to transport lithic materials cannot be assumed from these analyses. The movement of lithic materials may have been a simple "down the line" process of culling, transport, and reuse by Neanderthals. However, in the basal strata at La Quina only lithics of late-stage reduction are recovered suggesting that tool manufacture did not occur on site. In the upper beds, all stages of reduction have been identified and the raw material tends to be less heavily reduced. Sourcing of the La Quina materials will add greatly to our understanding of resource procurement patterns and mobility.

The variation in Middle Paleolithic lithic assemblages discerned here may represent two patterns of exploitation or two parts of the same subsistence pattern. Even and serrated edged tools appear to vary differently. Scraper rich industries, with high tool frequencies, may be the result of short-term foraging activities, while assemblages with higher percentages of denticulates, cores, and flakes may represent longer term occupation events. No domestic debris is found with imported scrapers, and scrapers are less commonly associated with the products of early stage manufacture. More analyses of the non-retouched tool component of Mousterian assemblages will be necessary to know if the patterns of tool morphology and intensity of reduction found at La Quina are typical in the Middle Paleolithic. Similar studies cited in Chapter II suggest that the variability recognized here is a widely dispersed pattern. These patterns will be explored further in the conclusion, Chapter VII.

CHAPTER VII

CONCLUSION

As discussed in Chapter II, a number of recent archaeological analyses have shown that the classic "form-function" debate over variations in retouched tool frequencies alone adds little to our understanding of Middle Paleolithic cultural variability. Rolland (1977, 1981), Dibble (1984, 1987a), Barton (1988, 1989) and Jelinek (1988a) have all shown that lithic tool morphology is not invariant but continuous in nature. Most of the tool types defined by Bordes (1961) can be grouped into sets of tools with even or serrated edges. The analysis of the Middle Paleolithic flake tools from La Quina suggest that this duality in edge form of retouched tools can be associated with variability in the rest of the lithic assemblage. The analysis of unretouched lithic artifacts at La Quina revealed that much of the variation in lithic manufacture and reduction can be correlated with tool edge form. Even edged tools in the basal strata arrived at La Quina in a preformed state. They were found with rejuvenation or retouch flakes and little other lithic material. These artifacts from late-stage lithic reduction were relatively intensively used. In contrast, denticulate tools with serrated edges were found in association with artifacts from all stages of manufacture in the upper beds. These lithics appear to be less intensively reduced than those from the lower beds. Climatological differences between the La Quina strata has been related to differences in the lithic assemblages. Evidence from other Paleolithic sites suggests that these correlations may be fairly widespread. Variation in raw material availability as well as reduction intensity have been used as evidence for changes in mobility. These patterns are used to discern changes in economy and settlement in the Paleolithic.

Studies by Fish (1979) and Dibble (1985) revealed that constraints of raw material availability were much better predictors of variation than tool classification. The sourcing of lithic materials from a number of archaeological assemblages has tied these raw material constraints to patterns of mobility (Geneste 1985, Roebroeks *et al.* 1988). Sourcing of raw materials has shown that objects transported over a greater distance are more likely to be reduced than are objects recovered nearby. The predominance of artifacts of late-stage reduction on materials that were transported, and the more expedient use of local raw material produces a duality in lithic assemblages. This differential use of raw material seem to be consistently present in Middle Paleolithic assemblages, although it cannot be conclusively related to a single cause. Changes in reduction technology can be explained by changes in adaptive strategy. As will be shown in the following examples, the effects of carrying costs manifest themselves in different ways in different environments.

The same patterns of lithic variation found at La Quina have been recognized by other researchers. Rolland's pioneering work (1977, 1981) showed that Middle Paleolithic variability in 120 assemblages could be related to implement frequencies and an opposition between scrapers and denticulates. He found that relative tool frequencies were high when scrapers were dominant in an assemblage, and that these frequencies were low when denticulates predominated. These differences in

reduction intensity were also recognized in the La Quina analysis. Secondly, Rolland found that scrapers were often produced on fine-grained stone, while denticulates and notched tools were made out of lesser quality material. Although he argued that these differences were due to functional requirements, the pattern may also be associated with differential mobility as suggested by the La Quina data. Finally, Rolland noted that in all but Denticulate assemblages, mean tool length exceeds that of flakes. The difference is particularly marked in Charentian assemblages. These size differences are similar to data collected from the La Quina sample which have been interpreted as resulting from differential intensity of raw material reduction. In the lower beds, retouch flakes from scrapers are markedly smaller than the imported, preformed tools. The difference between flake and tool size in the upper beds is less marked, suggesting that a more complete sequence of lithic reduction is present.

In their analyses of a number of Mousterian assemblages, Geneste (1985) and Meignen (1988) have also found patterns of variation similar to those recognized in the analyses of the La Quina material. They suggested that these patterns were tied to resource transport. Geneste (1985) analyzed the sources for a series of lithic assemblages from Southwest France (Aquitaine) and found that denticulate tools were often produced on local raw material. Artifacts from all stages of reduction were found fashioned out of this local, usually lesser quality, material. Non-local material invariably comprised a much smaller proportion of the total lithic assemblage. The artifacts on exotic materials were for the most part retouched tools (scrapers, Mousterian points and bifaces in particular) with few cores or by-products of early stage manufacturing. Although sourcing of raw materials from La Quina has not been included in this study, the patterns of exploitation and reduction appear to be similar to Geneste's findings.

A similar study by Meignen (1988) at the site of Marillac replicated the findings of Geneste. Denticulates and notches were fashioned from local material and occurred with cortical flakes and cores of the same material. 85 per cent of artifacts made from a higher quality exotic material were retouched tools. The remaining objects of this material were short-wide scraper retouch flakes similar to those found in the basal strata at La Quina.

This dual pattern of raw material exploitation can be seen in the collections from other Middle Paleolithic excavations as well. On the coast of Normandy at the site of Saint-Vaast-la-Hougue, the Mousterian assemblages have been divided into two general horizons (Roebroeks *et al.* 1988). In the lower strata, notched and denticulate tools were found with cores, cortical flakes, and poorly made scrapers. These artifacts were knapped on local material. In contrast, the assemblages from the upper beds were dominated by scrapers. Cores and cortical flakes were virtually absent. The raw material in these strata was a high quality flint obtained from at least 10 kilometers away.

Dibble, Roth, and Lenoir (1995) reached similar conclusions at Combe-Capelle Bas. The site sits on a flint source, so they were able to test the effects of raw material availability on lithic assemblages. Once again, Levallois flakes, tools, blades and non-cortical flakes tended to be made on non-local material. An equal number of cores were made on local and non-local material, but the exotic cores were more reduced. Dibble and Roth (1995) note that the typological makeup of local and imported tool assemblages at Combe-Capelle Bas is very similar, but more scrapers are more likely to be produced of exotic raw material. Imported tools were previously reduced at another site and appear to be more heavily reduced than tools made from local material.

Although few denticulate tools are recovered in "Pontian" Mousterian assemblages from Italy, Kuhn (1991) has found patterns of resource explotation at several sites there that are similar to La Quina. Kuhn analyzed lithic materials from two caves on the Tyrrhenian coast of Italy. At one site, . assemblages were primarily comprised of relatively reduced scrapers and informal cores. At the second site, more patterned cores and less reduced tools were recovered. The scraper-rich industries included a higher percentage of exotic material than the collections with less reduced tools. Kuhn suggests that raw material use was maximized at the latter site by the use of centripidal (disc) cores and unretouched flakes, while tools were more intensively utilized at the former site. The differences between these two cave sites replicate the variation found between the upper and lower strata at La Quina; where heavily reduced scrapers are found in opposition to more patterned cores and less heavily reduced tools.

Rolland and Dibble (1990) found many waste flakes, cores and tool blanks but few retouched tools or tool blanks at quarry sites in Northern France. These assemblages occurred on loess plateaus with easy access to flint nodules. In contrast, they found that assemblages recovered from enclosed sites frequently have more intensely reduced materials than those recovered at open air sites. Rolland and Dibble posit that a pattern of long distance migratory hunting during severe peniglacial conditions may have resulted in more intensive use of raw materials. Under milder climatic conditions, hunting was focused on more locally mobile and less migratory species. Raw material availability was more constant during these milder periods, and reduction was therefore less intense. The resulting assemblages are usually classified with Denticulate (and sometimes Typical) industries because of their prevalence of notched tools.

Barton's analysis (1988, 1989) of Middle Paleolithic assemblages from the Iberian Peninsula found variation in lithic morphology and reduction intensity that differs from that recognized in French artifacts of the same period. Assemblages from a series of upland sites contained relatively high frequencies of scrapers associated with higher frequencies of unretouched flakes than at lowland sites. Flint was reported to be easily obtainable near several of the upland sites and the majority of these recovered lithics were made of flint. Fewer lithics were found at the lowland sites and they were more heavily reduced. At some of the lowland sites flint was less

easily acquired and a majority of the artifacts were made out of material at hand, such as beach pebbles. Nevertheless, retouched tools still had a relatively high tendency to be fashioned out of flint. Many of the retouched tools in these lowland assemblages had "distinctive" edge shapes (notches, piercers, and burins); Barton interpreted these industries as reflecting short-term activity. A pattern of high mobility at the upland sites was proposed, with lowland sites representing longer occupation, lower mobility and diminished lithic replenishment. Although scrapers are associated with raw material sources and less intensive reduction here, higher quality, more distant raw material was still used in a more intensive manner than lesser quality, local resources.

Another pattern of raw material use was described by Schild and Sulgostowska (1988). They have suggested that the Rifle Range site 120 kilometers South-southeast of Warsaw at Zwolen was a game drive locality. Excavations recovered a limited number of lithic artifacts (n=56) with quantities of animal bone in an ancient ravine. Flint nodules were imported from a distance of 40 kilometers and shaped into bifaces on site. The other retouched tools, predominantly scrapers, were fashioned out of bifacial thinning flakes. Two Levallois flakes were also imported to the ravine. No cores were present. The low density of lithic artifacts and prevalence of even-edged tools at this site are interesting complements to the similar materials recovered at the base of the La Quina cliff face.

Although the duality in raw material reduction is often observed in the opposition of scrapers and denticulates/cores, relative frequencies of bifaces and other tool forms can also be shown to reflect differential raw material use. Flakes of rejuvenation of bifacial tools are often found in high numbers with few spent tools at a great distance from the raw material source. At Pech de l'Azé IV (Bed F4) few hand axes were found, but high numbers of bifacial retouch flakes were recovered. Of the 22,698 artifacts recovered, only four per cent are flake tools, .0004 per cent are bifaces (n = 8) and less than one per cent are cores. The percentages are similar from an MTA bed (Layer 4) at Pech I. Of the 35,100 artifacts collected: 71 per cent of them were biface retouch flakes, 11 per cent were retouched flake tools, .004 per cent were bifaces (n = 156) and less one than per cent were cores (Bordes 1972, 1978). Although these materials were not sourced to allow the reconstruction of mobility patterns, both of these assemblages have low relative frequencies of cores and retouched tools along with evidence of intensive reduction of even-edged tools.

Locus J at the site of Maastricht-Belvedere (Netherlands) contained several bifacial resharpening flakes but no bifacial tools. Roebroeks et al. (1988) infer that hand axes must have been part of a "mobile" toolkit retouched on site. A second example of displaced bifacial thinning flakes from this time period is found at the West German site of Plaidt-Hummerich. These flakes were recovered in excavations over 100 kilometers from their raw material source (Bosinski et al. 1986 cited in Roebroeks et al. 1988). These patterns of reduction on bifacial tools can be compared to Geneste's (1985) findings for the use of such implements in the Périgord. He discovered that bifaces were often curated and carried in a manner similar to scrapers.

Economizing behavior in the transport of prepared cores has also been recognized at Middle Paleolithic sites. In the Central Negev, Munday (1976) found that 90 per cent of variability in debitage size could be accounted for by factors of mobility. Eighty percent of core weight could also be accounted for by these factors. Artifacts exhibited more technological preparation when recovered at a greater distance from their source.

These patterns of raw material use from various sites in Europe repeatedly suggest that Middle Paleolithic hominids were utilizing finer quality raw materials in a different way than lesser quality materials. Although flint nodules were carried across the landscape in Poland, more highly valued resources were usually reduced at their source to be more easily transportable. The technology and morphology of the exotic artifacts exhibit traits of more patterned and intensive reduction. Artifacts recovered at a distance from their source are often found in the form of scrapers, bifaces and cores or debitage from these tools; these artifacts usually reflect more intensive use of raw material. On the other hand, locally available raw materials were often used to produce flakes and tools more expediently and less intensively.

Middle and Upper Paleolithic Comparisons

These data have also been used to address questions concerning the mental capacities of Middle Paleolithic hominids in relation to those of fully modern humans. This debate is based upon

> the question of whether or not the earlier
> hominids had already developed an
> adaptation functionally equivalent to that of
> modern *H. sapiens,* that is, whether or not
> their interactions with one another and with
> their environment were structured in
> essentially the same manner as those of
> modern humans, or whether Middle
> Paleolithic culture was somehow different in
> nature (Chase and Dibble 1987:264).

A series of papers and conferences have focused on this issue (Clark and Lindly 1989a, 1989b; Dibble 1989; Farizy 1990). Patterns of procurement, planning and mobility recognized in the analyses of the La Quina lithic assemblages can be seen to continue directly from the Middle to the Upper Paleolithic at other sites. This continuity implies that hominid interaction with the environment did not substantially change simultaneous with apparent changes in physiology.

In one example, Geneste (1988, 1990b) sourced lithic material from a number of Aurignacian and Périgordian assemblages for comparison with Middle Paleolithic data. He found that patterns of raw material acquisition did not dramatically change from the Middle to Upper Paleolithic, although foraging distances seemed to have increased over time. Changes in the expansion of hunter-gather territories and diversification of resource acquisition were more dramatic at beginning of the Middle Paleolithic than at its close.

Studies of a series of Italian Paleolithic sites by Kuhn (1992)

suggest that differences in technological planning among Middle and late Upper Paleolithic populations in that region may be explained in terms of contrasting patterns of land use. All of the sites considered have access to the same raw material and have comparable faunal remains, but late Upper Paleolithic assemblages have significantly larger quantities of non-local raw material, almost exclusively in the form of extensively modified tools. Kuhn does not believe the differences reflect a lack of planning ability by Neanderthals, but rather result from a more opportunistic, spatially diffused Mousterian adaptation than later in time. In fact, Stiner and Kuhn (1992) suggest that this shift in economy and settlement patterns occurs during the late Middle Paleolithic, at about 55,000 year ago, rather than at the Middle/Upper Paleolithic "break."

In the Upper Paleolithic strata at the site of La Riera in Spain, Clark (1989) found patterns of raw material use similar to those in the Middle Paleolithic of Southwestern France.

> Changes in the lithic procurement subsystem
> are roughly correlated with changes in
> dominant retouched tool types and/or
> relative amounts of knapping debris of
> different kinds (1989:40).

Notched tools and denticulates were found with relatively high numbers of cores and debitage. These were all made of locally available quartzite. In this region, flint nodules are relatively scarce and small. The flint assemblage at La Riera was primarily comprised of elaborately retouched tools and microliths with little associated debitage. Again, reduction intensity and carrying costs appear to have been at the center of the variability in raw material and tool morphology.

Analyses of the lithic assemblages from Laugerie-Haute by Demars (1987) have also shown patterns of transport in the Upper Paleolithic similar to those recognized in this study. Throughout the long archaeological sequence at Laugerie-Haute, Demars found that the majority of artifacts were consistently fashioned out of local material. Exotic flints from up to 50 kilometers away formed a small but significant part of the assemblages. These artifacts were often imported as products of blade manufacture. Better quality flint was used more economically and reduced more elaborately than local flint.

This analysis has shown that differences in tool morphology can account for much of the variability in Middle Paleolithic lithic assemblages. Serrated and even edged tools often occur in opposition to each other. Analyses of the non-retouched tool component of the La Quina assemblages showed that other classes of artifacts varied in association with these two tool groups. Scrapers were recovered only with products of late stage reduction (edge rejuvenation flakes), while denticulates were found with more cores, cortical flakes, and other early stage reduction debris. These patterns have been related to raw material transport. Carrying costs for more distant resources are suggested to be reflected in the importation of lithics with more preparation and reduction. Faunal and other environmental data suggest that the assemblages of previously reduced materials may be correlated with patterns of greater mobility and colder climatic regimes than assemblages containing a greater range of lithic reduction techniques and stages.

Sourcing of the materials included in this sample will shed additional light upon the patterns of mobility and raw material use recognized in this study. Detailed analysis of the cores from La Quina will help to further elucidate patterns of manufacture and reduction on this class of artifacts. More studies of Middle Paleolithic non-retouched lithic assemblages as well as retouched artifacts will confirm or clarify these patterns recognized at La Quina.

LA QUINA DATA ENTRY PROGRAM

SQUARE ID
LEVEL
CLASS
  FLAKE
  TOOL
  CORE
  CHUNK
MATERIAL /CLASS=FLAKE,TOOL,CORE,CHUNK
  FLINT
  QUARTZ
  JASPER
  OTHER
LONGITUDINAL PORTION /CLASS=FLAKE,TOOL,CHUNK
  WHOLE
  MEDIAL
  DISTAL
  PROXIMAL
LATITUDINAL PORTION /CLASS=FLAKE,TOOL,CHUNK
  WHOLE
  LEFT SPLIT
  RIGHT SPLIT
  LEFT BROKEN
  RIGHT BROKEN
CORTEX /CLASS=FLAKE,TOOL,CHUNK
  <10%
  10-40%
  40-60%
  60-90%
  >90%
LATERAL CORTEX /CLASS=FLAKE,TOOL,CHUNK
  LEFT
  RIGHT
  CENTER
PLATFORM CORTEX /CLASS=FLAKE,TOOL,CHUNK
  <10%
  10-50%
  50-90%
  >90%
PLATFORM SURFACE /CLASS=FLAKE,TOOL
  PLAIN
  TRANSVERSE
  DIHEDRAL
  STRAIGHT FACET
  CONVEX FACET
  REMOVED
  SHATTERED
  MISSING
DEVIATION/CLASS=FLAKE,TOOL
  CENTER (80-100)
  LEFT (40-80)
  STRONG LEFT (0-40)
  RIGHT (100-140)
  STRONG RIGHT (140-180)

TECHNIQUE /CLASS= FLAKE,TOOL,CORE
  NORMAL
  LEVALLOIS
  DISC-CORE (DISCOID)
  BIFACE RETOUCH
  SCRAPER RETOUCH
  DENTICULATE RETOUCH
  JANUS
  OTHER
FORM /CLASS= FLAKE,TOOL
  NORMAL
  ANGULAR
  LONG-FLAT
  OVOID/ROUND-FLAT
  LONG-THIN
  LONG-THICK
  SHORT-WIDE
  OVOID/ROUND
  TRIANGULAR
SCAR MORPHOLOGY /CLASS= FLAKE,TOOL
  1
  1 w/ retouch
  2
  2 w/ retouch
  3+
  3+ w/ retouch
  PLAIN
  CORTICAL
  CORTICAL w/ retouch
BORDES' TYPE /CLASS=TOOL
SECONDARY BORDES' TYPE /CLASS=TOOL
LENGTH /CLASS=FLAKE,TOOL
WIDTH /CLASS=FLAKE,TOOL
THICKNESS /CLASS=FLAKE,TOOL

Appendix II

ATTRIBUTE DESCRIPTIONS

Class : All artifacts were classified as flakes, tools, cores or chunks. Flakes are defined as lithic artifacts struck from parent rock with no further modification, while tools are characterized by the presence of modification. Cores are stone objects with one or more negative flake scars. Chunks have no strong positive or negative flake scars and no modification.

Material : All artifacts were defined as being made of flint, quartz (including quartzite), jasper or other material.

Longitudinal Portion : Flakes, tools and chunks were classified as being whole or broken (medial, distal or proximal portions).

Latitudinal Portion : Flakes, tools and chunks were classified as being whole, broken (left or right missing), or split (left or right missing).

Cortex : The exterior cortical coverage on flakes, tools and chunks was estimated and classified into one of 5 groups. The groups are: <10%, 10-40%, 40-60%, 60-90% or >90%. Tools with extensive modification of the exterior surface were placed in the "not applicable" class due to alteration of their exterior cortex.

Lateral Cortex : If any exterior cortex was present on a flake, tool or chunk, it was judged to be on the left right or center of the exterior surface.

Platform Cortex : The coverage of cortex on the platform surface of all flakes, tools and chunks was estimated and attributed to one of 4 ranges: <10%, 10-50%, 50-90% or >90%. If the platform of the artifact was altered or removed, it was attributed to the not applicable category.

Platform Surface : The surface of the platform for all flakes and tools was described by one of 8 categories. The groups are: plain, plain/transverse, dihedral, straight/faceted, convex/faceted, removed, shattered or missing.

Angle of Deviation : Flakes and tools were recorded as to the direction and amount of deviation. The point of maximum length of each whole artifact was measured on a radial graph with the bulb of percussion in the center and the plane of the striking platform on the 0°-180° axis. The degrees of the graph were divided into 5 categories : 0°-40° strong left, 40°-80° left, 80°-100° center, 100°-140° right, and 140°-180° strong right.

Technique : Flakes and tools were grouped into one of 9 classes. Each of the classes was defined by a number of technological and/or morphological attributes. The groups are : normal, Levallois, discoid, Janus, tool modification (biface, scraper or denticulate), other or not applicable. The technique for core reduction (Levallois, disc-core or normal) was also recorded.

Form : Flakes and tools were grouped into one of ten broad morphological classes : normal, angular, long-flat, ovoid/round-flat, long-thin, long-thick, short-wide, ovoid/round, triangular. Broken or modified artifacts were place in a "not applicable" category.

Scar Morphology : The exterior surface on flakes and tools was judged to fall into one of 12 classes: 1 scar, 1 with retouch, 2 flake scars, 2 with retouch, 3 or more flake scars, 3 or more with retouch, plain/no scar, cortical, cortical with retouch or not applicable.

Typology : All retouched artifacts were classified by Bordes (1961) typology. Tools were classified as to their primary and (if necessary) secondary type.

Metric Measurements : Measurements were taken with digital calipers on any flakes and tools whose original dimensions could be recorded. Broken flakes or tools with intensive retouch were not measured.

Length : A measurement of flake length was taken from the point of percussion along the axis of percussion to the point farthest from that point.

Width : A measurement of flake width was taken perpendicular to the length at the midpoint of the length.

Thickness : A measurement of flake thickness was taken perpendicular to both the length and the width at the midpoint of width.

REFERENCES

Ahler, S. A.

1989a Mass analysis of flaking debris. In *Alternative Approaches to Lithic Analysis*, edited by Henry and Odell, pp 85-118. Archaeological Papers of the Anthropological Association Number 1. Washington, D.C.

1989b Experimental knapping with KRF and midcontinent cherts. In *Experiments in Lithic Technology*, edited by Amick and Maudlin, pp 199-234. BAR International Series 528. BAR, Oxford.

Alimen, H.

1951 Indications climatiques reperables dans les couches mousteriennes de la Quina (Charente). *Sedimentation et Quaternaire* pp 159-171. CNRS, Bordeaux.

Amick, D. S. and R. P. Mauldin

1989 Comments on Sullivan and Rozen's "Debitage analysis and archaeological interpretation". *American Antiquity* 54(1):166-168.

Armand, D.

n.d. Paleontologie. In *Rapports de synthese sur les fouilles de la Quina: fouilles 1985-1994*, edited by Debenath and Jelinek. Report to the French Ministry of Culture.

Bamforth, D. B.

1985 The technological organization of Paleo-Indian small-group bison hunting on the Llano Estacado. *Plains Anthropologist* 30:243-58.

1986 Technological efficiency and tool curation. *American Antiquity* 51:38-50.

Barbour, E. H. and C. B. Schultz

1932 The Scottsbluf Bison Quarry and its artifacts. *Bulletin of the Nebraska State Museum* 1:283-286. Lincoln.

Barnes, A. S. and H. H. Kidder

1936 Differentes techniques de debitage á la Ferrassie. *Bulletin de la Société Préhistorique Française* 33:272-288.

Barton, C. M.

1988 *Lithic Variability and Middle Paleolithic Behavior*. BAR International Series #408. BAR, Oxford.

1989 Beyond style and function: A view from the Middle Paleolithic. *American Anthropologist*.

1991 Retouched tools, fact or fiction? Paradigms for interpreting Paleolithic chipped stone. In *Perspectives on the Past: Theoretical Biases in Mediterranean Hunter-Gatherer Research*, edited by Clark, pp 143-163. University of PA Press, Philadelphia.

Baumler, M. F.

1988 Core reduction, flake production, and the Middle Paleolithic industry of Zobiste (Yugoslavia). In *Upper Pleistocene Prehistory of Western Eurasia*, edited by Dibble and Montet-White, pp 255-274. University Museum, Philadelphia.

Baumler, M. F. and C. E. Downum

1989 Between micro and macro: A study in the interpretation of small-sized lithic debitage. In *Experiments in Lithic Technology*, edited by Amick and Maudlin, pp 101-116. BAR International Series 528. BAR, Oxford.

Beyries, S.

1987 *Variabilite de l'industrie lithique au Mousterien*. BAR International Series 328. BAR, Oxford.

1988 Functional variability of lithic sets in the Middle Paleolithic. In *Upper Pleistocene Prehistory of Western Eurasia*, edited by Dibble and Montet-White, pp 213-223. University Museum, Philadelphia.

Binford, L. R.

1973 Interassemblage variability: the Mousterian and the functional arguement. In *The Explanation of Culture Change*, edited by Renfrew, pp 227-254. Duckworth, London.

1980 Willow smoke and dog's tails: Hunter-gatherer settlement systems and archaeological site formation. *American Antiquity* 45:4-20.

1983 *Working at Archaeology*. Academic Press, New York.

Binford, L. R. and S. R. Binford

1966 A preliminary analysis of functional variability in the Mousterian of Levallois facies. *American Anthropologist* 68(2):238-295.

Binford, S. R. and L. R. Binford

1969 Stone tools and human behavior. *Scientific American.* 220:70-84.

Binford, L. R. and J. A. Sabloff

1982 Paradigms, systematics, and archaeology. *Journal of Anthropological Research* 38:137-153.

Binford, S. R.

1968a Variability and change in the Near Eastern Mousterian of Levallois facies. In *New Perspectives in Archaeology*, edited by Binford and Binford, pp 49-60. Aldine, Chicago.

1968b Early Upper Pleistoene adaptations in the Levant. *American Anthropologist* 70:707-717.

Boëda, E. and A. Vincent

1990 Role plausible de l'os dans la chaine de production lithique á La Quina: Donnes experimentales. Paper presented at "Les Mousteriens Charentiens", Brive, France.

Bordes, F.

1947 Etude comparative des différentes techniques de taille du silex et des roches dures. *L'Anthropologie* 51:1-29.

1950a Principes d'une méthode d'etude des techniques de débitage et de la typologie du Paléolithique Ancien et Moyen. *L'Anthropologie* 54:19-34.

1950b L'Evolution buissonnante des industries en Europe occidentale: Considerations theoretiques sur le Paléolithique Ancien et Moyen. *L'Anthropologie* 54:393-420.

1953 Essai de classification des industries "mousteriennes". *Bulletin de la Société Préhistorique Française* 50:457-466.

1954 Les gisements du Pech-de-L'Azé (Dorgogne): Le Moustérien de tradition Acheuleenne. *L'Anthropologie* 58:401-432.

1955 Les gisements du Pech-de-L'Azé (Dorgogne): Le Moustérien de tradition Acheuleenne. *L'Anthropologie* 59:1-38.

1961 *Typologie du Paléolithique ancien et moyen*. Delmas, Bordeaux.

1962 Le Moustérien á denticulés. *Arheoloski Vestnik* 13:43-49.

1966 Mousterian cultures in France. In *New Roads to Yesterday*, edited by Caldwell, pp 78-94. Basic Books, New York.

1968 *The Old Stone Age*. McGraw Hill (World University Library), New York.

1969 Reflections on typology and techniques in the Paleolothic. *Artic Anthropology* 6:1-29.

1972 *A Tale of Two Caves*. Harper and Row, New York.

1978 Typological variability in the Mousterian layers at Pech de L'Aze I, II, and IV. *Journal of Anthropological Research* 34:181-193.

Bordes, F. and M. Bourgon

1951 Le complexe Moustérien: Moustériens, Levalloisien et Tayacien. *L'Anthropologie* 55:1-23.

Bordes, F. and D. de Sonneville-Bordes

1970 The significance of varibility in Paleolithic assemblages. *World Archaeology* 2:61-73.

Bordes, F., J.-Ph. Rigaud and D. de Sonneville-Bordes

1972 Des buts, problemes et limites de l'archeologie paléolithique. *Quaternaria* 16:15-34.

Boule, M.

1911 L'homme fossile de la Chapelle-aux-Saints. *Annals de Paleolontologie* 6:111-172.

1912 L'homme fossile de la Chapelle-aux-Saints. *Annals de Paleolontologie* 7:85-190.

1913 L'homme fossile de la Chapelle-aux-Saints. *Annals de Paleolontologie* 8:1-70.

Breuil, H.

1913 Les subdivisions du Paléolithique superieur et leur signification. *Congres International d'Anthropologie et d'Archaeologie Préhistorique*, 1912 Geneva, pp 165-238.

1932 Les industries á eclats du paléolithique ancien. *Préhistoire* 1: 125-190.

Breuil, H. and L. Koslowski

1931 Etudes de stratigraphie dans le Nord de la France, la Belgique et l'Angleterre. *L'Anthropologie* 41:449-488.

Burton, J.

1980 Making sense of waste flakes: New methods for investigating the technology and economics behind chipped stone assemblages. *Journal of Archaeological Science* 7:131-148.

Champion, T., C. Gamble, S. Shennan and A. Whittle

1984 *Prehistoric Europe*. Academic Press, London.

Chang, K. C.

1986 *The Archaeology of Ancient China*. 4th edition. Yale University Press, New Haven.

Chase, P.G.

n.d. Paleontology.. In *Rapports de synthese sur les fouilles de la Quina: fouilles 1985-1994*, edited by Debenath and Jelinek. Report to the French Ministry of Culture.

Chase, P. G. and H. L. Dibble

1987 Middle Paleolithic symbolism: A review of current evidence and interpretations. *Journal of Anthropological Archaeology* 6:263-296.

Chauvet, G.

1896 *Bulletin de la Société archéologique et historique de la Charente*. Angouleme.

1897 *Stations quaternaires de la Charente*. Angouleme.

Clark, G. A.

1988 Some thoughts on the Black Skull: An archaeologists's assessment of WT-17000 (*A. boisei*) and systematics in human paleontology. *American Anthropologist* 90(2):357-371.

1989 Romancing the stones: Biases, style and lithics at La Riera. In *Alternative Approaches to Lithic Analysis*, edited by Henry and Odell, pp 27-50. Archaeological Papers of the Anthropological Association Number 1. Washington, D.C.

Clark, G. A. and J. M. Lindly

1989a The case for continuity: Observations on the biocultural transition in Europe and western Asia. In *The Human Revolution: Behavioral and Biological Perspectives on the Origins of Modern Humans*, edited by Mellars and Stringer, pp 626-676. Edinburgh University Press, Edinburgh.

1989b Modern human origins in the Levant and western Asia: The fossil and archaeological evidence. *American Anthropologist*: 91:962-985.

Clark, J. D.

1968 Studies of hunter-gatherers as an aid to the interpretation of prehistoric societies. In *Man the Hunter*, edited by Lee and DeVore, pp 276-280. Aldine, Chicago.

Clark, J. D. and M. R. Kleindienst

1974 The Stone Age cultural sequence: Terminology, typology and raw material. In *Kalambo Falls Prehistoric Site*, Vol 2, edited by Clark, pp 71-106. Cambridge University Press, Cambridge.

Close, A. E.

1989 Identifying style in stone artifacts. In *Alternative Approaches to Lithic Analysis*, edited by Henry and Odell, pp 3-26. Archaeological Papers of the Anthropological Association Number 1. Washington, D.C.

Copeland, L.

1975 The Middle and Upper Paleolithic of Lebanon and Syria in light of recent research. In *Problems in Prehistory: North Africa and the Levant*, edited by Wendorf and Marks, pp 317-350. SMU Press, Dallas.

Cotterell, B. and J. Kaminga

1987 The formation of flakes. *American Antiquity* 52:675-708.

Cowgill, G.

1968 Archaeological applications of factor, cluster and proximity analysis. *American Antiquity* 33:367-375.

Daniel, G.

1950 *A Hundred Years of Archaeology*. Duckworth, London.

Debénath, A.

1976 Les civilizations du Paléolithique moyen en Charente. In *La Préhistoire Française*, edited by de Lumley, pp 1070-1076. Editions du CNRS, Paris.

Debénath, A. and A. J. Jelinek

1985 Rapport sur la campagne de fouilles 1985 á La Quina.

1987 Rapport sur la campagne de fouilles 1987 á La Quina.

1990 La Quina: Campagnes 1988-1990.

Delpech, F. and E. Donard, A. Gilbert, J.-L. Guadelli, O. LeGall A. Martini-Jacquin, M.-M. Paquereau, F. Prat, J.-F. Tournépiche

1983 Contribution á la lecture des paleoclimats quaternaires d'apres les donnes de la paleontologie en mileu continental. *Paléoclimats* 34:165-177. CNRS, Bordeaux.

Demars, P. Y.
1987 L'economie du silex á Laugerie Haute (Dordogne). Paper given at the Vth International Flint Symposium, Bordeaux.

Dibble, H. L.
1984 Interpreting typological variation of Middle Paleolithic scrapers: function, style or sequence of reduction. *Journal of Field Archaeology* 11:431-436.

1985 Raw-material variation in Levallois flake manufacture. *Current Anthropology* 26:391-393.

1987a The interpretation of Middle Paleolithic scraper morphology. *American Antiquity* 52(1):109-117.

1987b Measurement of artifact provenience with an electric theodolite. *Journal of Field Archaeology* 14:249-254.

1988 Typological aspects of reduction and intensity of utilization of lithic resources in the French Mousterian. In *Upper Pleistocene Prehistory of Western Eurasia*, edited by Dibble and Montet-White, pp 181-198. University Museum, Philadelphia.

1989 The implications of stone tool types for the presence of language during the Lower and Middle Paleolithic. In *The Human Revolution*, edited by Mellars and Stringer, pp 415-432. Edinburgh University Press, Edinburgh.

1995 Raw Material Availability, Intensity of Utilization, and Middle Paleolithic Assembalge Variability. In *The Middle Paleolithic Site of Combe-Capelle Bas*, edited by Dibble and Lenoir. University Museum, Philadelphia.

Dibble, H.L. and M. Lenoir
1995 *The Middle Paleolithic Site of Combe-Capelle Bas*. University Museum, Philadelphia.

Dibble, H.L. and B. Roth
1995 Raw Material Use at Combe-Capelle Bas, Dordogne, France. Paper presented at the Paleoanthropology Meeetings, Oakland, CA.

Dibble, H.L., B. Roth and M. Lenoir
1995 The Use of Raw Matierials at Combe-Capelle Bas. In *The Middle Paleolithic Site of Combe-Capelle Bas*, edited by Dibble and Lenoir, pp 179-207. University Museum, Philadelphia

Dibble, H. L. and J. C. Whittaker
1981 New experimental evidence on the relation between percussion flaking and flake variation. *Journal of Archaeological Science* 8:283-296.

Dunnell, R. C.
1978 Style and function: A fundamental dichotomy. *American Antiquity* 43:192-202.

Farizy, C.
1990 *Paléolithique Moyen Recent et Paléolithique Superieur Ancien en Europe*. Memoires du Musée de Préhistoire d'Ile en France No. 3, CNRS, Nemours.

Fish, P.
1978 Consistency in archaeological measurement and classification: A pilot study. *American Antiquity* 43:86-89.

1979 The interpretive potential of Mousterian debitage. *Arizona State University Anthropological Research Papers* 16.

1981 Beyond tools: Middle Paleolithic debitage analysis and cultural inference. *Journal of Anthropological Research* 37:374-386.

Fladmark, K. R.
1982 Microdebitage analysis: Initial considerations. *Journal of Archaeological Science* 9:205-220.

Freeman, L. G., Jr.
1964 Mousterian developments in Cantabrian Spain. Unpublished Ph.D. dissertation, Dept. of Anthropology, The University of Chicago.

1966 The nature of Mousterian facies in Cantabrian Spain. *American Anthropologist* 68:9-21.

1968 A theoretical framework for interpreting archaeological materials. In *Man the Hunter*, edited by Lee and DeVore, pp 262-267. Aldine, Chicago.

Frison, G. C.
1968 A functional analysis of certain chipped stone tools. *American Antiquity* 33(2)149-155.

Geneste, J.-M.
1985 Analyse lithique d'industries moustériennes du Périgord. Thesis, University of Bordeaux.

1988 Systemes d'approvisionment en matiers premiers au Paléolithique moyen et au Paléolithique superieur en Aquitaine. In *L'Homme de Néandertal: La Mutation* (V8), edited by Kozlowski, pp 61-70. Etudes et Recherches Archéologiques de la Unversité de Liège, Liège.

1989 Economie des ressources lithiques dans le Moustérien du Sud-Ouest de la France. In *L'Homme de Néandertal: La Subsistance* (V6), coordinated by Patou and Freeman, pp 75-97. Etudes et Recherches Archéologiques de la Unversité de Liège, Liège.

1990a Les industries de la Grotte Vaufrey: Technologie du débitage, economie et circulation de la matiere premiere lithique. In *La Grotte Vaufrey á Cenac et Saint-Julien*, edited by Rigaud, pp 441-517. Société Préhistorique Française, Paris.

1990b Developpement des systems de production lithique au cours du Paléolithique moyen en Aquitaine Septentrionale. In *Paléolithique moyen recent et Paléolithique superieur ancien en Europe*, edited by Farizy, pp 203-213. Memoires du Musée de Préhistoire d'Ile de France No. 3. CNRS, Nemours.

Geneste, J.-M. and J.-Ph. Rigaud
1989 Matieres premieres lithiques et occupation de l'espace. In *Variations des Paléomilieux et Peuplement Préhistorique*, edited by Laville, pp 205-218. CNRS, Paris.

Grayson, D. K.
1983 *The Establishment of Human Antiquity*. Academic Press, New York.

1986 Eoliths, archaeological ambiguity, and the generation of "Middle Pange" research. In *American Archaeology Past and Future*, edited by Meltzer et al, pp 77-133. Smithsonian Insitution, Washington.

Guillien, Y. and G. Henri-Martin
1974 Criossance du renne et saison de chasse: Le

moustérien á denticules et le moustérien de tradition acehuleenne de La Quina. *Inter-nord* 13-14: 119-127.

Hayden, B. and W. K. Hutchings
1989 Whither the billet flake? In *Experiments in Lithic Technology*, edited by Amick and Maudlin, pp 235-257. BAR International Series 528. BAR, Oxford.

Henri-Martin, G.
1964 La derniere occpation moustérienne da La Quina, Charente: Datation par la radiocarbone. *C. R. Academie Science Paris* 258:3533-3535.
1966 Decouverte d'un temporal humain neandertalien dans le moustérien de La Quina, Charente. *C. R. Academie Science Paris* 262:1937-1939.
1969 La Quina. In *Livret-Guide de l'Excursion á Berry-Poitou-Charentes*, pp 91-95. INQUA, Paris.
1976 La Quina. In *Livret-Guide de l'Excursion á Berry-Poitou-Charentes*, pp 158-162. INQUA, Paris.

Henri-Martin, H.
1907 *Recherches sur L'Evolution du Moustérien dans le gisement de La Quina (Charente)* Premier Fascicule. Schleicher Freres, Paris.
1909 *Recherches sur L'Evolution du Moustérien dans le gisement de La Quina (Charente)* Deuxième Fascicule. Schleicher Freres, Paris.
1923a *L'Homme Fossile de la Quina*. Librarie Octave Doin, Paris.
1923b *Recherches sur l'evolution du moustérien de la Quina (Charente) (V4): Industrie Lithique*. Angouleme.
1936 Comment vivait l'homme da La Quina á l'epoque moustérienne. *Préhistoire*, pp 7-23. Leroux, Paris.

Henry, D. O., C. V. Haynes and B. Bradley
1976 Quantitative variations in flaked stone debitage. *Plains Anthropologist* 21:57-61.

Henry, D. O. and G. H. Odell
1989 Preface. In *Alternative Approached to Lithic Analysis*, edited by Henry and Odell, pp ix-xi.

Holdoway, S., S. McPherron and B. Roth
n.d. A Proposed Resharpening Sequence for Notched Tools in Western European Lower and Middle Paleolithic Assemblages.

Hublin, J. J.
1980 A propos de restes inedits du gisement de La Quina (Charente). *L'Anthropologie* 84:81-88.

Issac, G.
1968 The Acheulian site complex at Olorgesailie, Kenya. Unpublished Ph.D. dissertation, University of Cambridge.

Jelinek, A. J.
1965 Lithic technology conference, Les Ezyies, France. *American Antiquity* 31:277-278.
1966 Some distinctive flakes and flake tools from the Llano Estecado. *Papers from the Michigan Academy of Science, Arts, and Letters* Vol. L1, pp 399-405.
1975 A preliminary report on some Lower and Middle Paleolithic industries from the Tabun Cave, Mount Carmel (Israel). In *Problems in Prehistory: North Africa and the Levant* edited by Wendorf and Marks, pp 297-315. SMU Press, Dallas.

1976 Form, function, and style in lithic analysis. In *Cultural Change and Continuity*, edited by Cleland, pp 19-33. Academic Press, New York.
1977a A preliminary study of flakes from the Tabun Cave, Mount Carmel. *Eretz-Israel* 13:87-96
1977b The Lower Paleolithic: Current evidence and interpretations. *Annual Review of Anthropology* 6:11-32.
1982a The Tabun Cave and Paleolithic man in the Levant. *Science* 216:1369-1375.
1982b The Middle Paleolithic in the Southern Levant, with comment on the appearance of modern *Homo sapiens*. In *The Transition from the Lower to the Middle Paleolithic and the Origin of Modern Man*, edited by Ronen, pp 57-101. BAR International Series 151. BAR, Oxford.
1987 The 1987 La Quina excavation season: A brief report of activities conducted under NGS Grant 3524-87.
1988a Technology, typology, and culture in the Middle Paleolithic. In *Upper Pleistocene Prehistory of Western Eurasia*, edited by Dibble and Montet-White, pp 199-212. University Museum, Philadelphia.
1988b A report on the National Geographic Society Excavations at La Quina (Charente), France in 1986-1988.
1990a Excavations at the Middle Paleolithic site of La Quina. NSF Proposal.
1990b *Problems in the chronology of the Middle Paleolithic and the first apprearance of early modern Homo sapiens in Southwest Asia*. Paper presented at "The Evolution and Dispersal of Modern Humans in Asia" Tokyo, November 14-17, 1990.
1991 Observations on reduction patterns and raw materials in some middle Paleolithic industries in the Pérogord. In *Raw Material Economies among Prehistoric Hunter-Gatherers*, edited by Montet-White and Holen, pp 7-31. University of Kansas Publications in Anthropology #19, Lawrence.
n.d. The lithic industries. In *Rapports de synthese sur les fouilles de la Quina: fouilles 1985-1994*, edited by Debenath and Jelinek. Report to the French Ministry of Culture.

Jelinek, A. J., A. Debénath and H. L. Dibble
1989 A preliminary report on evidence related to the interpretation of economic and social activities of Neandertals at the site of La Quina (Charente) France. In *L'Homme de Néandertal: La Subsistance* (V6), coordinated by Patou and Freeman, pp 99-106. Etudes et Recherches Archéologiques de la Unversité de Liège, Liège.

Jelinek, A. J., W. R. Farrand, G. Haas, A. Horowitz and P. Goldberg
1973 New excavations at the Tabun Cave, Mt Carmel, Israel, 1967-1972: a preliminary report. *Paleorient* 1:151-183.

Jones, G. T., C. Beck and D. K. Grayson
1989 Measures of diversity and expedient lithic technologies. In *Quantifying Diversity in Archaeology*, edited by Leonard and Jones, pp 69-78. Cambridge University Press, Cambridge.

References

Keeley, L. H.
1980   *Experimental Determination of Stone Tools Uses.* Univeristy of Chicago Press, Chicago.

Kelly, R. L.
1985   Hunter-gatherer mobility strategies. *Journal of Anthropological Research* 39:277-306.
1988   The three sides of a biface. *American Antiquity* 53(4):717-731.

Kelly, R. L. and L. C. Todd
1988   Coming into the country: early Paleo-Indian hunting and mobility. *American Antiquity* 53:231-244.

Kuhn, S. L.
1990   A geometric index of reduction for unifacial stone tools. *Journal of Archaeological Science* 17:583-593.
1991   "Unpacking reduction: lithic raw material economy in the Mousterian of West-Central Italy. *Journal of Anthropological Archaeology* 10: 76-106.
1992   On planning and curated technologies in the Middle Paleolithic. *Journal of Anthropological Research* 48(3):185-214.
1994   A formal approach to the design and assembly of mobile toolkits. *American Antiquity* 59(3):426-442.

Lartet, E. and H. Christy
1864   Cavernes du Périgord. *Revue Archaeologique* 1:233-267.

Laville, H.
1964   Recherches sédimentologiques sur la paloclimatologie du Würmien recent en Périgord. *L'Anthropologie* 68:1-48.
1973   *Climatologie et Chronologie du Paléolithique en Périgord: Etude sédimentologique de dépots en Grotte et sous Abris.* Unpublished PhD dissertation, Insitute de Quaternaire, Université de Bordeaux I.
1975   *Climatologie et chronologie du Paléolithique en Périgord.* Memoir 4, Etudes Quaternaires. Editions du Laboratoire de Paléontologie Humaine et de Préhistoire, Université de Provence.
1988   Recent developments on the chronostratigraphy of the Paleolithic in the Périgord. In *Upper Pleistocene Prehistory of Western Eurasia,* edited by Dibble and Montet-White, pp 147-160. University Museum, Philadelphia.

Laville, H., J.-Ph. Rigaud and J. Sackett
1980   *Rock Shelters of the Périgord: Geological Stratigraphy and Archaeological Succession.* Academic Press, New York.

Laville, H. and J.-L. Turon, J.-P. Texier, J.-P. Raynal, F. Delpech, M.-M. Paquereau, F. Prat, A. Debénath
1983   Histoire Paléoclimatique de l'Aquitaine et du Golfe de Gascogne au pleistocene superieur dupuis le dernier interglaciare. *Paléoclimat* 34: 219-241. CNRS, Bordeaux.

Lenoir, M.
1973   Obtention experimentale de la retouche de type Quina. *Bulletin de la Société Préhistorique Française* 70:10-11.
1986   Un mode d'obtention de la retouche Quina dans le Moustérien de Combe Grenal. *Bulletin de la Société Anthropologique du Sud-Ouest* 21:153-160.

Leroi-Gourhan, A.
1956   La galerie moustérienne de la grotte du renne (Arcy-sur-Cure, Yonne). *Congrès Préhistorique de France* (1956):1-16.
1961   Les fouilles d'Arcy-sur-Cure (Yonne). *Gallia Préhistoire* 4:3-16.

Lindly, J. M. and G. A. Clark
1990   Symbolism and modern human origins. *Current Anthropology* 31:233-261.

Magne, M.
1989   Lithic reduction stages and assemblage formation processes. In *Experiments in Lithic Technology,* edited by Amick and Maudlin, pp 15-32. BAR International Series 528. BAR, Oxford.

Magne, M. and D. Pokotylo
1981   A pilot study in bifacial lithic reduction sequences. *Lithic Technology* 10:34-47.

Marks, A. E.
1975   An outline of prehistoric occurences and chronology in the Central Negev, Israel. In *Problems in Prehistory: North Africa and the Levant,* edited by Wendorf and Marks, pp 351-362. SMU Press, Dallas.
1983   The Middle to Upper Paleolithic transition in the Levant. in *Advances in World Archaeology,* Vol 2, edited by Wendorf and Close, pp 51-98.
1988   The curation of stone tools during the Upper Pleistocene. In *Upper Pleistocene Prehistory of Western Eurasia,* edited by Dibble and Montet-White, pp 275-286. University Museum, Philadelphia.
1989   Early Mousterian settlement patterns in the Central Negev, Israel: Their social and economic implications. In *L'Homme de Néandertal: La Subsistance* (V6), coordinated by Patou and Freeman, pp 115-126. Etudes et Recherches Archéologiques de la Unversité de Liège, Liège.

Marks, A. E. and D. A. Friedel
1977   Prehistoric settlement patterns in the Avdat/Aqev area. In *Problems in Prehistory: North Africa and the Levant,* edited by Wendorf and Marks, pp 131-154. SMU Press, Dallas.

Maudlin, R. P. and D. S. Amick
1989   Investigating patterning in debitage from experimental bifacial core reduction. In *Experiments in Lithic Technology,* edited by Amick and Maudlin, pp 67-88. BAR International Series 528. BAR, Oxford.

McCown, T. and K. Kennedy
1972   *Climbing Man's Family Tree: A Collection of Major Writings of Human Phylogeny.* Prentice Hall, Englewood Cliffs, N.J.

Meignen, L.
1988   Un exemple de comportement technologique différentiel selon les matieres premières: Marillac, couches 9 et 10. In *L'Homme de Néandertal: La Technique* (V4), edited by Binford and Rigaud, pp 71-79. Etudes et Recherches Archéologiques de la Unversité de Liège, Liège.

Meignen, L. and B. Vandermeersch
1986   Le Gisement de Marillac (Charente). *111 Congrés national des Sociétés savantes, Pre- et Protohistoire,* pp 135-144.

Meignen, L. and O. Bar-Yosef
1988 Variabilite technologique au Proche Orient: L'example de Kebara. In *L'Homme de Néandertal: La Technique* (V4), edited by Binford and Rigaud, pp 81-95. Etudes et Recherches Archéologiques de la Unversité de Liège, Liège.

Mellars, P. A.
1969 The chronology of Mousterian industries in the Périgord region of South-west France. *Proceedings of the Prehistoric Society* 35:134-171.

1970 Some comments on the notion of functional variability in stone tool assemblages. *World Archaeology* 2:74-89.

1986 A new chronolgy for the French Mousterian period. *Nature* 322:410-411.

1988 The chronology of the South-west French Mousterian. In *L'Homme de Néandertal: La Technique* (V4), edited by Binford and Rigaud, pp 97-119. Etudes et Recherches Archéologiques de la Unversité de Liège, Liège.

Morrow, C.A.
1984 A biface production model for gravel-based chipped stone industries. *Lithic Technology* 13:20-29.

Mortillet, G. de
1883 *Le Préhistorique: Antiquité de l'Homme*. Reinwald, Paris.

Munday, F.C.
1976 Intersite variability in the Mousterian of the Central Negev. In *Prehistory and Paleoenvironments in the Central Negev*, edited by Marks, pp 113-140. SMU Press, Dallas.

1977 Nahal Aqev (D35): a stratified, open-air Mousterian occupation in the Avdat/Aqev area. In *Prehistory and Paleoenvironments in the Central Negev*, edited by A.E. Marks, pp 35-54. SMU Press, Dallas.

1979 Levantine Mousterian technological variability: a perspective from the Negev. *Paleorient* 5:87-104.

Newcomer, M.H.
1971 Some quantitative experiments in handaxe manufacture. *World Archaeology* 3:85-94.

Odell, G.H.
1981 The morphological express at function junction: Searching for meaning in lithic tool types. *Journal of Anthropological Research* 37:319-342.

Owen, W. E.
1938 The Kombewa Culture, Kenya Colony. *Man* 218:203-205.

Parry, W. J. and R. L. Kelly
1987 Expedient core technology and sedentism. In *The Organization of Core Technology*, edited by Johnson and Morrow, pp 285-304. Westview Press, Boulder.

Patterson, L.W. and J.B. Solberger
1978 Replication and classification of small size lithic debitage. *Plains Anthropologist* 23:103-112.

Patou, M.
1989 Subsistance et approvisionnement au Paléolithique Moyen. In *L'Homme de Néandertal: La Subsistance* (V6), coordinated by Patou and Freeman, pp 11-18. Etudes et Recherches Archéologiques de la Unversité de Liège, Liège.

Peyrony, D.
1930 Le Moustier, ses gisements, ses industries, ses couches geologiques. *Revue Anthropologique* 1-3:48-76 and 4-6.

1934 La Ferrassie. *Préhistoire* 3:1-92.

Renault-Miskovski, J.
1990 L'environment vegetal des mousteriens charentiens. Paper presented at "Les Mousteriens Charentiens", Brive, France.

Rigaud, J.-Ph. and J.-M. Geneste
1990 L'utilization de l'espace dans la Grotte Vaufrey. In *La Grotte Vaufrey á Cenac et Saint-Julien*, by Rigaud, pp 593-611. Société Préhistorique Française, Paris.

Roebroeks, W., J. Kolen and E. Rensink
1988 Planning depth, anticipation and the organization of Middle Paleolithic technology. *Helinium* 28:17-34.

Rolland, N.
1977 New aspects of Middle Paleolithic variability in Western Europe. *Nature* 266:251-252.

1981 The interpretation of Middle Paleolithic variability. *Man* 16:15-42.

1988a Variabilite et Classification. In *L'Homme de Néandertal: La Technique* (V4), edited by Binford and Rigaud, pp 169-183. Etudes et Recherches Archéologiques de la Unversité de Liège, Liège.

1988b Observations on some Middle Paleolithic time series in Southern France. In *Upper Pleistocene Prehistory of Western Eurasia*, edited by Dibble and Montet-White, pp 161-180. University Museum, Philadelphia.

Rolland, N. and H. L. Dibble
1990 A new synthesis of Middle Paleolithic variability. *American Antiquity* 55:480-499.

Rozen, K. C. and A. P. Sullivan
1989 Measurement, method, and meaning in lithic analysis: problems with Amick and Mauldin's middle-range approach. *American Antiquity* 54(1):169-175.

Sackett, J. R.
1973 Style, function and artifact variability in Paleolithic assemblages. In *The Explanation of Culture Change*, edited by Renfrew, pp 317-325. Duckworth, London.

1981 From de Mortillet to Bordes: A century of French Paleolithic archaeology. In *Towards a History of Archaeology*, edited by Daniel, pp 85-99. Thames and Hudson, London.

1986 Isochretism and style: A clarification. *Journal of Anthropological Archaeology* 5:266-277.

Scheider, F.
1972 An analysis of waste flakes from sites in the Upper Knife-Heart Region, North Dakota. *Plains Anthropologist* 17:91-100.

Schiffer, M. B.
1972 Archaeological context and systemic context. *American Antiquity* 37:156-175.

1987 *Formation Processes of the Archaeological Record*. University of New Mexico Press, Albuquerque.

Schild, R. and Z. Sulgostowska
1988 The Middle Paleolithic of the Northern European Plain at Zwolen. In *L'Homme de Néandertal: La Mutation* (V8), edited by Kozlowski, pp 149-167.

Etudes et Recherches Archéologiques de la Unversité de Liège, Liège.

Shackleton, N. J. and N. D. Opdyke
1973 Oxygen isotope and paleomagnetic stratigraphy of equatiorial Pacific core V28-238. *Quaternary Research* 3:39-55.

Sheets, P. D.
1975 Behavioral analysis and the structure of a prehistoric industry. *Current Anthropology* 16:369-391.

Speth, J. D.
1972 Mechanical basis for percussion flaking. *American Antiquity* 37:34-60.

Stahle, D. W. and J. E. Dunn
1982 An analysis and application of size distribution of waste flakes from the manufacture of bifacial stone tools. *World Archaeology* 14:84-97.

Stiner, M.C. and S.L. Kuhn
1992 Subsistence, technology, and adaptive variation in Middle Paleolithic Italy. *American Anthropologist* 94:306-339.

Stringer, C. and C. Gamble
1993 *In Search of the Neanderthals*. Thames and Hudson, New York.

Sullivan, A. P. and K. C. Rozen
1985 Debitage analysis and archaeological interpretation. *American Antiquity* 50(4)755-779.

Tavoso, A.
1984 Reflexion sur l'économie des matieres premières au Moustérien. *Bulletin de la Société Préhistorique Française* 81:79-82.

Texier, J.-P. and J.-P. Raynal, H. Laville, M.-m. Paquereau, F. Prat, A. Debénath, F. Delpech
1983 Histoire paléoclimatique de l'Aquitaine du pleistocene ancien au dernier interglaciare. *Paléoclimat* 34:207-217. CNRS, Bordeaux.

Thomas, D. H.
1989 Diversity in hunter-gatherer cultural geography. In *Quantifying Diversity in Archaeology*, edited by Leonard and Jones, pp 85-91. Cambridge University Press, Cambridge.

Thomas, D. H. and S. L. Bierwirth
1983 Projectile points and additional stone tools. In *The Archaeology of Monitor Valley 2. Gatecliff Shelter* by Thomas, pp 177-224. Anthropological Papers of the American Museum of Natural History Vol 59:1.

Toth, N.
1985 Archaeological evidence for preferential right-handedness in the Lower and Middle Pleistocene, and its possible implications. *Journal of Human Evolution* 14:607-614.
1987a The first technology. *Scientific American* 265(4):112-121.
1987b Behavioral inferences from early stone artifact assemblages: An experimental model. *Journal of Human Evolution* 16:763-787.

Turq, A.
1987 *Exploitation des Matieres Premieres Lithiques dans Le Mousterien entre Dordogne et Lot*. Paper given at the 5th International Flint Colloquium, Bordeaux.

Vandermeersch, B.
1976 Les neandertaliens en Charente. In *La Préhistoire Française*, edited by de Lumley, pp 584-587. CNRS, Paris.

Valladas, H., J.-M. Geneste, J. L. Joron and J. P. Chadelles
1986 Thermoluminescence dating of Le Moustier (Dordogne, France). *Nature* 322:452-454.

Valladas, H., J. Chadelle, J. Geneste, J. Joron, L. Meignen, P. Texier
1987 Datations par la thermoluminescence de gisements moustériens du Sud de la France. *L'Anthropologie* 91:211-226.

Verjux, C.
1988 Les denticulés Moustériens. In *L'Homme de Néandertal: La Technique* (V4), edited by Binford and Rigaud, pp 197-204. Etudes et Recherches Archéologiques de la Unversité de Liège, Liège.

Villa, P.
1983 *Terra Amata and the Middle Paleolithic Archaeological Record of South France*. University of California Press, Berkeley.

Webb, R. E.
1988 The implications for Middle Paleolithic culture history of recent attempts at radiometric dating. In *L'Homme de Neandertal: La Chronologie* (V1), coordinated by Patou and Freeman, pp 125-134. Etudes et Recherches Archéologiques de la Unversité de Liège, Liège.

White, A. M.
1963 Analytic description of the chipped-stone industry from Snyders site, Calhoun Co, Illinois. *Anthropological Papers* #19, pp 1-70. Museum of Anthropology, University of Michigan.

White, R.
1985 *Upper Paleolithic Land Use in the Périgord*. BAR International 253, Oxford.

Wiant, M. D. and H. Hassen
1984 The role of lithic resource availability and accessibility in the organization of lithic technology. In *Lithic Resource Procurement* edited by Vehik, pp 101-114. Center for Archaeological Investigations Occasional Paper 4, Southern Illinois University.

Wiessner, P.
1985 Style or isochrestic variation? A reply to Sackett. *American Antiquity* 50:160-166.

Wilmsen, E. N.
1970 Lithic analysis and cultural inference: A Paleo-Indian case. *University of Arizona Anthropological Papers* #16.

Wu, R. K. and J. W. Olsen (editors)
1985 *Paleoanthropology and Paleolithic Archaeology in the People's Republic of China*. Academic Press, Orlando.

Young, D. and D. B. Bamforth
1990 On the macroscopic identification of used flakes. *American Antiquity* 55:403-409.

www.ingramcontent.com/pod-product-compliance
Lightning Source LLC
Chambersburg PA
CBHW061304270326
41932CB00029B/3469